Bible
Interpretations
Twentieth Series
April 5 – June 28, 1896

Luke

Bible Interpretations

Twentieth Series

Luke

These Bible Interpretations were published in the Inter-Ocean Newspaper in Chicago, Illinois during the late eighteen nineties.

By
Emma Curtis Hopkins

President of the Emma Curtis Hopkins Theological Seminary at Chicago, Illinois

WISEWOMAN PRESS

Bible Interpretations: Twentieth Series

By Emma Curtis Hopkins

© WiseWoman Press 2014

Managing Editor: Michael Terranova

ISBN: 978-0945385-71-4

WiseWoman Press

Vancouver, WA 98665

www.wisewomanpress.com

www.emmacurtishopkins.com

CONTENTS

Editors Note

All lessons starting with the Seventh Series of Bible Interpretations will be Sunday postings from the Inter-Ocean Newspaper in Chicago, Illinois. Many of the lessons in the following series were retrieved from the International New Thought Association Archives, in Mesa, Arizona by, Rev Joanna Rogers. Many others were retrieved from libraries in Chicago, and the Library of Congress, by Rev. Natalie Jean.

All the lessons follow the Sunday School Lesson Plan published in "Peloubet's International Sunday School Lessons". The passages to be studied are selected by an International Committee of traditional Bible Scholars.

Some of the Emma's lessons don't have a title. In these cases the heading will say "Comments and Explanations of the Golden Text," followed by the Bible passages to be studied.

Foreword

By Rev. Natalie R. Jean

I have read many teachings by Emma Curtis Hopkins, but the teachings that touch the very essence of my soul are her Bible Interpretations. There are many books written on the teachings of the Bible, but none can touch the surface of the true messages more than these Bible interpretations. With each word you can feel and see how Spirit spoke through Emma. The mystical interpretations take you on a wonderful journey to Self Realization.

Each passage opens your consciousness to a new awareness of the realities of life. The illusions of life seem to disappear through each interpretation. Emma teaches that we are the key that unlocks the doorway to the light that shines within. She incorporates ideals of other religions into her teachings, in order to understand the commonalities, so that there is a complete understanding of our Oneness. Emma opens our eyes and mind to a better today and exciting future.

Emma Curtis Hopkins, one of the Founders of New Thought teaches us to love ourselves, to

speak our Truth, and to focus on our Good. My life
has moved in wonderful directions because of her
teachings. I know the only thing that can move me
in this world is God. May these interpretations
guide you to a similar path and may you truly
remember that "There Is Good For You and You
Ought to Have It."

Introduction

Emma Curtis Hopkins was born in 1849 in Killingsly, Connecticut. She passed on April 8, 1925. Mrs. Hopkins had a marvelous education and could read many of the worlds classical texts in their original language. During her extensive studies she was always able to discover the Universal Truths in each of the world's sacred traditions. She quotes from many of these teachings in her writings. As she was a very private person, we know little about her personal life. What we do know has been gleaned from other people or from the archived writings we have been able to discover.

Emma Curtis Hopkins was one of the greatest influences on the New Thought movement in the United States. She taught over 50,000 people the Universal Truth of knowing "God is All there is." She taught many of founders of early New Thought, and in turn these individuals expanded the influence of her teachings. All of her writings encourage the student to enter into a personal relationship with God. She presses us to deny anything except the Truth of this spiritual Presence in every area of our lives. This is the central focus of all her teachings.

The first six series of Bible Interpretations were presented at her seminary in Chicago, Illinois. The remaining Series', probably close to thirty, were printed in the Inter Ocean Newspaper in Chicago. Many of the lessons are no longer available for various reasons. It is the intention of WiseWoman Press to publish as many of these Bible Interpretations as possible. Our hope is that any missing lessons will be found or directed to us.

I am very honored to join the long line of people that have been involved in publishing Emma Curtis Hopkins's Bible Interpretations. Some confusion exists as to the numbering sequence of the lessons. In the early 1920's many of the lessons were published by the Highwatch Fellowship. Inadvertently the first two lessons were omitted from the numbering system. Rev. Joanna Rogers has corrected this mistake by finding the first two lessons and restoring them to their rightful place in the order. Rev. Rogers has been able to find many of the missing lessons at the International New Thought Alliance archives in Mesa, Arizona. Rev. Rogers painstakingly scoured the archives for the missing lessons as well as for Mrs. Hopkins other works. She has published much of what was discovered. WiseWoman Press is now publishing the correctly numbered series of the Bible Interpretations.

In the early 1940's, there was a resurgence of interest in Emma's works. At that time, Highwatch Fellowship began to publish many of her writings, and it was then that *High Mysticism*, her seminal work was published. Previously, the material contained in High Mysticism was only available as individual lessons and was brought together in book form for the first time. Although there were many errors in these first publications and many Bible verses were incorrectly quoted, I am happy to announce that WiseWoman Press is now publishing *High Mysticism* in the a corrected format. This corrected form was scanned faithfully from the original, individual lessons.

The next person to publish some of the Bible Lessons was Rev. Marge Flotron from the Ministry of Truth International in Chicago, Illinois. She published the Bible Lessons as well as many of Emma's other works. By her initiative, Emma's writings were brought to a larger audience when DeVorss & Company, a longtime publisher of Truth Teachings, took on the publication of her key works.

In addition, Dr. Carmelita Trowbridge, founding minister of The Sanctuary of Truth in Alhambra, California, inspired her assistant minister, Rev. Shirley Lawrence, to publish many of Emma's works, including the first three series of Bible Interpretations. Rev. Lawrence created mail order courses for many of these Series. She has graciously passed on any information she had, in order to assure that these works continue to inspire individuals and groups who are called to further study of the teachings of Mrs. Hopkins.

Finally, a very special acknowledgement goes to Rev Natalie Jean, who has worked diligently to retrieve several of Emma's lessons from the Library of Congress, as well as libraries in Chicago. Rev. Jean hand-typed many of the lessons she found on microfilm. Much of what she found is on her website, www.highwatch.net.

It is with a grateful heart that I am able to pass on these wonderful teachings. I have been studying dear Emma's works for fifteen years. I was introduced to her writings by my mentor and teacher, Rev. Marcia Sutton. I have been overjoyed with the results of delving deeply into these Truth Teachings.

In 2004, I wrote a Sacred Covenant entitled "Resurrecting Emma," and created a website, www.emmacurtishopkins.com. The result of creating this covenant and website has brought many of Emma's works into my hands and has deepened my faith in God. As a result of my love for these works, I was led to become a member of Wise-Woman Press and to publish these wonderful teachings. God is Good.

My understanding of Truth from these divinely inspired teachings keeps bringing great Joy, Freedom, and Peace to my life.

Dear reader; It is with an open heart that I offer these works to you, and I know they will touch you as they have touched me. Together we are living in the Truth that God is truly present, and living for and through each of us.

The greatest Truth Emma presented to us is "My Good is my God, Omnipresent, Omnipotent and Omniscient."

Rev. Michael Terranova

WiseWoman Press

Vancouver, Washington, 2010

LESSON I

The Radiation Of Light

Luke 13:22-30

The subject of this lesson is "The Radiation of Light." It necessitates mentioning some practical illustrations in order to make plain how the divine light shines. The international committee on Bible Lessons declare that the subject of today is "Warning Against Sin." They also give some practical illustrations to explain their meanings. For instance, they say, "There comes a time when it is too late, when no hope of entering is written over the door. Age comes on. The opportunities flee away and do not return. It is not a joy for Christ to see men thus thrust out. He longs for them to enter in," etc.

The Bible verses on which we all base our meditations are found in Luke 13:22-30.

The golden text reads: "Strive to enter in at the straight gate." The words are from a discourse of Jesus while on his Perean round of preaching. As

1

Perea means "beyond," "extended," "farther on," etc., suppose we take it for a hint that as he was preaching in Perea he meant for us to go beyond the usual explanations of his sayings and dip our oars into the sunny waters of that land beyond the sky into which his own eyes were always gazing.

If we do this we find ourselves breathing from on high. We feel that there is sunshine in our veins and not blood. We feel our feet touching new foundations. Taking interpretations farther on in beauty than the committee should permit, we find that Jesus Christ knew a way of living that never had any closing down of hope, feeble age, whimpering Christ, etc. He knew of a city whose gates are never closed. He told of a door which no man could shut. He set the unlimited before us. He set the unspeakable close to the tip of our tongues. He opened up the heavenly highway.

Contemplating Jesus Christ's sermon as here recorded, by going far beyond the committee's permissions, we find a life-giving breath doth breathe us upward as on pinions. We do not have the sad impressions which the doctrine of no hope, closed opportunities, decrepit winding up, as mostly preached, do most certainly give.

Souls Shall Not Disappear
As this will be about the only spot on earth today where the actual Perean meaning will be taken in hand, let us do it thoroughly. Let us make the bold proclamation that Jesus Christ meant by this sermon that it is doctrines that shall fall down

and disappear and not the soul of man anywhere or by any name. Let us make the far reaching, endless announcement that he was really telling that nothing can ever close down on you or me or our neighbors; neither death, nor age, nor hope, nor opportunities. Let us stretch the wings of our message to the extent of declaring that he was really saying that the gnashing of teeth is all to be done by the tumbling doctrines of the trials and sufferings and darkness of man as preached by the most sincere pulpit orators of past generations.

Have we not found that angels are the sincere thoughts of good men, as they formulate themselves across the face of the wonderful God? Have we not read that to confess Jesus Christ in preference to thinking good thoughts is to get on our own triumphing base quickest? Have we not been told that the godliest men are those who have most artfully hidden the true light from our faces? Have they not graven their images across the face of the Father while best describing him?

Last Sunday's lesson is the mate to this. Without it we cannot so quickly tell what this one means. It told of how we can become sensitized film for any sort of flying principles to print themselves on.

It brought up Wellington as a sensitized plate for receiving the determination of the nations against Napoleon, and how the very sun and moon of human mind had to stand still or move on for his well-prepared forces when they rose up.

3

It shows what a non-committal state of mind did for Joshua when it got to acting. He had the power to say: "Sun, stand thou still upon Gibeon; and thou, moon, in the valley of Aijalon. And the sun stood still, and the moon stayed. "It brought up Paderewski as an example of negative mental in the presence of musical principles. It brought up Jesus as declining to receive their kind of forces and turning the other way to get his charges of power. He let his own Me charge him and his be-ing from itself as center through all his extremities; through his flesh and clothes, through his thoughts and his subtle influences stealing through time and nations.

He spoke of making himself, his divine Me, the charge with which he would empower himself.

Cared for No Worldly Honors

He did not care to be a great musician. He did not care to be a great financier. He did not care to be a soldier. He did not care to be land holder or a mill owner. He saw that to be himself was all he had to do.

So he knew nothing. He deliberately knew nothing. He did it on purpose. He did nothing. He deliberately did nothing. He kept still on purpose. He had no will. He dropped it on purpose. He had no friends. He let them forsake him on purpose. He had no possessions. He let them go on purpose. He was thinking on purpose. He was fightless on purpose. So he was able to stand naked of mind, naked of will, naked of friendships, and thus be nothing but his unhampered self.

It came to charge his whole presence up so with beauty and radiance and beneficence that people were actually afraid of him.

Today's lesson tells of the radiation of the divine "I Am" through all the earth. It tells how miserably good for nothing all the principles are for which men have let themselves get entangled. How cheap is the fight and win-or-die theory. It cannot do anything when the fightless Me charges any of us up. How silly is the born-to-die theory when the deathless Me charges any one of us up. How like folly the lifetime spent in getting the symphonies, sonatas, and requiems when once the soundless choirs of enrapturing God are caught from the ever-present Me at the center of every creature.

And this is what today's lesson means. It goes with the other discourse of the mighty Jesus in which we find this passage: "If thine eye be single; thy whole body shall be full of light." That "eye" is without doubt, the personal pronoun "I". Let man have only one "I" to attend to and his whole realm shall glow with its character. So after telling them last Sunday to confess him in precredence to the theories of men, it is very fitting that he shall show how the divine Me thus confessed doth dispread itself abroad throughout the villages, cities, river sides, all tracks, and plains, wherever the stars or the others abide. (Verse 22)

5

Jerusalem Means "I Am"

He even says that while first attending to the Me it begins to shine over our earth. For Jerusalem always means the "I Am". And that verse 22 declares that as his attention was toward his Me, he did a wonderful deal of teaching and healing.

Stretching the verses to the heights and the lengths of their meaning we have it repeated how much preferable over all other things it is to be sensitized "I Am" in the presence of our own all-powerful Me.

For we, at that point, are all-wise, all-powerful, all-capable. Does anybody think the war spirit that charged Wellington with a lucky feeling, the harmonious spirit that kept Paderewski swinging forth tones is comparable to the might and splendor of the "I Am" that Jesus told us to charge up with? So, he said: "Strive to enter in at the straight gate." (Verse 24)

Look to the one only Me. Let everything else drop repent, turn back; catch what it does, says, or is; catch nothing else. This being the only way makes it a "straight" way. This is simple. It makes it narrow. That is the whole of being what you really are and shedding its glorious beams on your world, is narrowed down in being one who knows nothing, thinks nothing, and fights not, while your original nature is charging you up.

Many think to get into the consciousness of their original glory by trying to sit still like the adepts of India, or make themselves negative like the rare moments of the fighters of earth, but the whole thing is narrowed down to repentance and forgiveness.

By forgiveness is meant giving instead of; giving for. Given from on high the light and warmth of God to melt the hardness of earth. By this forgiveness from on high we radiate sunshine from that something which we really are in the beauty and majesty and sweetness of our first self. Nothing else counts. Let all else gnash and lash and fade itself to nothing.

God Has Compassion For Us

Then shall those doctrines of men wherein we have been taught how God loved to make things terrible in the first place and then dreaded so to see us get into his traps and networks of pain, all begin to see, most plausible. (Verse 26)

It is not reasonable that it is a difficult task to get home to our Father- Mother, God? This must be the doctrine of salvation. So, whoever shall preach this, he shall, of course, feel that he has been consistent with truth. (Verse 30)

That is a bogus I Am which says it is hard to get home to God. It must perish. The actual preaching of Jesus was that it is easy to step in the right track, because there is only one track to step in. All the rest seem to be tracks, but they lead nowhere. As there is only one "I Am" for all mankind to be, or see, or feel, so there is only one direction to go, one place to be. This fact makes it "straight."

7

Of course all the doctrines of men are against this. They say there is a hell to get into, a darkness to avoid, great dangers to shy away from. Of course the way to get our Father's hand has been called hard. Of course to be in divine power, divine in ability, divine in motherly givings, divine in resources from whence to draw plenty and plenty, and plenty, has been called hard. But calling it so does not make it so.

The International Committee quote Professor Peabody of Harvard University as saying that the harder they made their examination papers the more students they had. This is said to be the chief reason why we have had moiling and toiling, weeping and creeping, discouragement and faltering. In trying to get hold of the divine God. It is not discussed how it would have been with us if it had been perpetually dinned into our ears that the way is easy and the Father-Mother tenderness very, very near.

We can set up a system of thought and get many people to live by it, even while it is all fallacy. One man went out of his mind because the blower of the horn on his tally-ho coach failed to appear. That clique to which he belonged has a principle that if things were not in style, fashion, they should be everlastingly disgraced.

It is a principle of conduct nowadays that, if money is secured by the action society shall smile. If money is lost by it, society shall frown. While any of these principles are flourishing, they shall seem plausible enough. But flourishing like green bay trees does not make them Jesus Christ powers. So, the principle dinned for generations about the terrible hardships about a journey toward a faraway heaven, has a flourishing hold. It seems to be a fact. It is like Shakespeare's judgments according to appearances. Was he not called wonderfully smart because he used a fine set of artistically arranged words to describe human nature trained to think and believe against the Jesus Christ way?

There Is No Difficulty

"We have eaten and drunk in thy presence, and thou hast taught in our streets," say all the flourishing doctrines. Every I Am that talks a single proposition about there being any difficulty in touching, seeing, living the divine I Am, is a humbug — a hocus pocus. The instant the One I Am that is here is preached, it is found that all the talking machines that have sounded their din on our ears since over time set up its tunes shall cease.

And, according to this lesson, putting it with the other, they shall make their proudest yells just as they are orally perishing. In the deep heart of man he is for peace. When he begins to talk he has to talk like his neighbors. He touches the talk plans, "I am for peace. But when I speak, they are for war," said David.

There is a key of David. Many have wondered what it can be. This lesson makes it plain that it is a sure key to something beyond the pale of human experience for us to cease from talking on any subject whatsoever and be at one with that peace place within the universal heart. "I am for peace, but when I speak they are for war." Was the deep heart of David unlike the deep heart of other men? No; it is the flourishing of speech on the winds of time that finally makes quarrels and competitions.

The hurricane and the thunder tried to convince Elijah that they were the voice of the divine heart in all men. But, though he himself liked killing and torturing other men, arguing and orating against them like hurricane winds, he saw that he was not comforted at all. It was not by success in worrying against other prophets that his heart's depths were touched. It was not by windy eloquence that his hearts depths were touched. It was by some unwanted rest on the foundation place in the heart's everlasting peace.

Whoever interprets Jesus Christ as intimating that men and women shall wail because they cannot find their Father-Mother God is stopping wide of Perea. Whenever trying to explain the words of him of the open door, let the farthest stretches of expression we can find he made. They shall fall short of what the man knew. Let the earliest proclamations be made that can be concerning the easily reached Father God. They shall fall far wide of the sweet ease of the journey. Let the doctrine of hardship wail and gnash as it falters out of the mind of man. Strive to enter in at the straight gate, for many doctrines are claiming to lead heavenward but they lead nowhere.

There is truly but one way, and that is the easy way. How easy to rest from their labors and let the works follow the rest. How easy to stop orating and arguing and let the still place win its own laurels. How easy to stop thinking and let the light of the original Me shed its wisdom, charging radiance abroad.

Inasmuch as the doctrine of hardship, struggle, striving, end of hope, death, and a sorrowful Jesus Christ has led us nowhere, let us cease from its nonsense and lie down on the all-powerful, all accomplishing peace of the Jesus who longs for nothing because he owns everything.

The Inter Ocean Newspaper, April 5, 1896

Lesson II

The Great Supper

Luke 14:15-24

Let not the people forget that each one of these lessons will describe their personal experiences, for the work to which it belongs in that mission which their spiritual receptivity arranges.

Today's lesson, for instance, tells you to keep up your courage through the approaching ordeal of having your best efforts slighted. Be greater than your environments. Be stronger than the coming succession of bad news. Since you are great and stronger than your circumstances can possibly show up, it is your privilege to rise up and exhibit your greatness and strength.

The subject of this meditation is, "The Great Supper." The golden text is, "Come for all things are now ready."

The chapter and set of verses are, Luke 14:15-24. The place where the parable was told was Perea. The time when Jesus originated the theme was January, A.D, 30. It was meant that whenever it should be read in after ages it should touch the experience of whoever should read it. It was also meant as an address to the majesty inherent within all readers of the story.

The metaphysicians teach that if we address the nobility within men they will respond by exhibiting nobility. They also teach that if the majesty always present in men is addressed, they are certain to do something majestic.

All the discourses of Jesus were addressed to the greatness within us, and that is why his sermons are all so inspiring. It accounts for the great hold they have on the civilized world. For even animals and children prefer to be spoken to with respect and commendation.

It is recorded that Jesus talked sometimes to serpents and generations of vipers; also to devils. This is said by learned men to confess that Jesus saw vipers and devils. Those who know how pungent and dissolving to shades and mists our sun can be, say that Jesus was shining his glory on the shiny doctrines of this world, and in the pungent quality of his voice they disappeared from their homes in the mind of men then and there.

They cannot help believing that from the time he dissolved the silly doctrines of this world, men have had to fight and quarrel like cats and dogs to hold up those doctrines. The true doctrines would not need to be fought and quarreled for. It would have a potentiality about itself that would cause it to defend men rather than compel men to defend it. (Verse 23)

Speaking of doctrines once Jesus said: "Ye shall know the truth and the truth shall make you free." You will please notice that there is no hint in this proclamation about your making the truth free.

Those who watch the majesty and nobility in their neighbors have shining happy faces. Those who watch for the cheating or wicked streaks in them have dark, scowling countenances. Is it not plain that if Jesus always saw the face of his Father, and told all his hearers that the same Father was in them, he was telling the false doctrines that there was a hasty dissolution of them then and there when he said, "Ye serpents, generation of vipers, who hath warned you to flee from the wrath to come?" Of course, nobody had told the truth in their presence, and therefore they had had no signals of their coming disappearance.

Since he said those words there have been a great number of those old vipers clung unto by mankind, but the doctrines had their fangs extracted and their substance cremated when he let his face shine in their sight. So it has been mere memories to which mankind have been clinging and not the originals.

As an instance of hanging on to the ashes of a viper, let us notice the doctrine of God's anger at the wicked, his grief at sin, his longing for man to behave himself. This is taught from every so-called Christian pulpit in this very age.

It was in high moments of sight of truth that the prophets of old said, "God is of purer eyes than to behold iniquity." If God beholdeth not my iniquity, but only my shining immaculate soul, he certainly is not worried about my getting to paradise. This was the fact preached by Jesus to us all as offspring of Jehovah, and it is hanging on to fragments of folly to preach a disappointed or angry or vicious God, on the keen scent after my sins.

What the Lesson Teaches

This lesson is a call to look at the hidden, unconscious causes of outward movements. There is always a reason why you are stern with your children, or savage with your laundress, deeper than the mere action of today, while you are punishing them. Secretly you fear that if you are not strict with the children they will grow up badly; or if you do not scold the laundress she will bring in poor work again.

This fear may not have been an expression in your conscious mind. It is a hidden viper or doctrine. The same is true of the conduct of society. Why do the strong brained keep the weak-brained toiling in noisome mines, climbing giddy steeples, diving dangerous deeps? Do they not pay the lowest wages they can possibly hire them for? What secret reason prompts such unjust usage of their fellow men? It is because if they are not kept poor, starvation poor, they will not perform these menial tasks. What makes civilization? Is it the use of the terrified weak by the pompous strong? Do not dodge this hidden viper. Face him and see how substantial is the cause for the use of the masses. See what a glorious fact runs its eternal glory close to the slimy shade. Jesus preached that eternal glory. He said: "God careth, provideth, doeth wonders, bringeth heaven on earth, maketh all things new."

The lesson of today opens with verse 15: "And when one of them that sat at meat with him heard these things he said: Blessed is he that shall eat meat in the kingdom of God."

He meant to say to Jesus that he should like to see one man who could get his bread straight from the Father; his clothes straight from the city of kindness; his education straight from the Holy Ghost; his home directly from the many-mansioned house, all of which Jesus had said was possible to be done by anybody and everybody.

Then Jesus went on to say that this great supper of beneficence would never be tasted by that part of any of us which hurries and bustles and drives around trying to do things. Only that part of us which is despised and cornered into neglect can taste of this happy fact.

There are promptings within us that our hustling nature declares are dangerous to our well being. Up rises within us a wish to see all the children of this world equally happy. We crush back the wise because men have taught us that it is this very difference of happiness that makes this world so marvelous. That the dark sorrows of the down-trodden are as the background of some wonderful picture whose foreground is brilliant light.

Such teaching is bidden to stop still and sit down at a table where no such bread is ever of-fered. But such teaching says that if we could not be scrambling after joy we should not get married to get it (verse 20). "We should not buy low and sell dear to get it (verse 18). We should not whip and thrash to show our authority, and so get a morsel of it. In short, that there would be nothing to scramble for if we already had what we are scrambling after.

So, said Jesus, you would make scrambling the summum bonum (the highest good) but I say unto you, it is the finished supper, the table all spread, that is the happy state.

The peace of the heart once tasted, the whole outer man becomes happy, harmonious, free. The majesty of the eternal man once touched the whole outer man shows majesty. The nobility of the original character once spoken to, the whole con-duct of life is glorious.

The whole ministry of Jesus was to bring the great supper into sight. The most ragged should be clothed, because they should first see the entranc-ing robes of their divine soul. The hungriest should be fed, because they should first eat the divine substance.

Men Still Persist in Sinning

To this day we find men hanging on to the shade of the viper of that instruction once sent out from the pulpits of an ancient past, that it is coarse and material to speak of having the naked clothed here on this earth, because they ought to be satisfied with nature's obvious distinctions in brain, and fate's obvious distinction in fortune.

This is a preaching which even our youngest children reject. They do not like such eating. But, after being crammed with it, a few years they get convinced that there is no other fact in life practical.

That early, deep-seated antagonism to being made an underling or donkey is the prompting which Jesus says shall see the supper prepared, and eat of it as a practical experience right here on this so-called material plane.

There shall be no doctrine of the need of quelling our neighbors — have any food. There shall be no doctrine of the necessity for unhappiness to trim us into goodness — have anything to eat. There shall be no doctrine of the killing of oxen, or chickens, or lambs, as the appointed way of life — have anybody to agree with it to keep it going.

There shall be no doctrine of one man a pauper and one man a land man — have anybody to countenance it, and so keep it on its feet. Read verse 24; "None of those which were bidden shall taste of my supper." But the crowded- down instincts of tenderness shall eat and smile. The hushed up compassions shall eat and have enough to give forth wherever they move.

The secret wish to help every one that asks for help shall find sustenance sufficient to make it a reservoir of plenty, which cannot end. All people want to believe this. But they make excuses against it. Not because their soul approves of their arguments, but because they were taught to argue that way.

So Jesus makes a parable to tell us that the deep wishes, the deep wants, the deep compassions, are to rise up in some man or some woman and make him or her to find the Jesus Christ table at which the poor, the maimed, the blind, shall be compelled to eat, because, when the bruised and cornered compassions arise and eat then all those people on our streets who are they living pictures of our heart's best wishes as they are crowded back within us, shall be fed.

And there will be no need for them to cringe and flinch to the millionaires, begging to polish their boots. And there will be no need to cry at the gates of the stock yards for a chance to earn a penny. And there will be no need to buy land and sell land to get gold to buy clothes for our children.

And the Lord, in that day, shall do a strange thing, said Isaiah. Of course, to the hustlers and bustlers it will be strange. But to the heart's deepest choices it will be natural. To the deep heart's promptings the ways of this world on its outer planes, are strange. To those people who have let their hearts guide their lives unknowing of the all-supplying table at which they might feed and get enough and to spare, this world of business has been a strange land. How can we sing the Lord's song in such a strange land? We have hanged our harps on the willows, and by the rivers we have sat down to mourn.

But, the voice of the Master is heard in our streets. Rise, he calleth thee. The Lord hath provided a table here in our midst.

This is idealism. Perea asks us to preach Jesus deeper and grander than outer movements would warrant. Thus we must preach idealism. But even these interpretations, at their most idealistic stretches, fall far short of-what can be done for him who feeds his heart's promptings with the actual substance that is here, which, when the inner heart tastes, the outer life must fulfill. With the taste of this wonder bread in the soul, the outer tables are compelled to be visibly loaded.

With the beauty of the inner joy the outer faces must shine. With the handling of the heavenly goods by the inner heart's confidence the management of outer lands and houses and breads and beds must come. "The without shall be as the within," said Jesus. "Not so," urges the church. The doctrine of plenty and happiness on the outer plane is fought down, but Jesus preached it. The coming of one with enough of soul risen from the hidden deeps of his being, to rouse up the soul in a world full, is not believed in. But Jesus preached it. The end of having to push and crowd and try for ourselves is not supposed to have been reached. But, though Jesus was driven out of the coasts, or external life, once, He cometh there again, and this time he stays on the coast.

Inter-Ocean Newspaper, April 12, 1896

LESSON III

The Radiation Of Joy

Luke 15:11-24

Today's Bible lesson has for its theme, "The Radiation of Joy." It has for its personal, special announcement the proposition that we each have two external faculties, one of which is responsible for our chasing up and down, round about, everywhere, to try to find joy, and the other is responsible for nothing at all.

The way Jesus of Nazareth told this fact about the externals of human beings was by a parable of two sons; one went chasing and tearing up and down, the other stayed stupidly at home. Neither one was happy. (Luke 15:11¬24)

The idea is to show that there is actual joy in striking the Father point, the home base, whatever that may be. The Father base is evidently not the locus standi (place to stand) of the elder son who whined at what he called home, and it certainly is not anywhere that the hustling, arriving, investigating younger son took up his position.

Referring to a planetary state, Jesus meant to teach that the nerveless, grumpy Oriental has not touched the heart center any more than the excitable, scrambling Occident. The Father point, the heart center, the glad base, is something different from anything that either the sleepy Eastern religions have taught, or the crazy Western ones have screeched.

Making a personal application he meant to teach our conscious and subconscious external mind that the actual is nothing at all like either of them, even when they are behaving in most exemplary fashion.

For my thoughts are not your thoughts, neither are my ways your ways saith the Lord.

Yet, said Jesus, who himself had tried both ways, here is tremendous joy for both the wild, civilized West and the tame, self-hypnotized East, by attention to the actual. There is great personal delight for each man's external life by knowing how to run his conscious and subconscious mind backward toward the starting point, which is forever the same.

There is a gaze which is capable of bringing a flood of gladness down its channels; there is a name of the starting point which can act on life's coasts, or daily affairs, like sunshine on growing corn. There is no shame in finding that starting

point and feeling the world and our personal affairs transform by its influence. For all this plant
as it swings, and all our affairs as they run, are
like objects in the night. The lily is as black as the
ground in the night. The rose is as dark as the
mud in the evening. They are all dark. But let the
sun shine on them and there is a great transfor-
mation at once. Yet they never changed at all. So,
everything on this earth has been called unreal
and opposite to spirit because everything is waiting for the sun. Let that sun shine on them all and
will still be what they are, yet they will seem different.

Once when Jesus of Nazareth was giving this
same lesson he caused the investigating mind to
hurry to the ultimate on the external plane and
see where it would end. It ran down violently into
swine and then raced into the sea. No matter what
line we are running on we come out as swine and
perish by drowning. The pleasure seeker has as
hard a time as the religious preacher. And certainly there is no more discouraged specimen of
humanity than the religious preacher who at-
tempts to go out and put his theories into practice
in the extremists fashion. He has to agree with
Parkhurst that the world is a bad lot. He has to
throw himself on the floor in despair at the impos-
sibility of helping humanity, as did an ardent
young Christian missionary.

Lesson From Tiberius

Tiberius tried power at its ultimate stretch. He wrote to his servile Senate: "All the gods and goddesses are daily tormenting me."

Solomon tried school books at their farthest stretches; he tried religious, metaphysics also at their profoundest statements; he tried money in extreme amounts. But both Tiberius with sensual pleasure, and Solomon, with religion and school lore, ran into the state of mad swine and then were drowned. A caliph heard Solomon groaning in anguish while in the swine era: "I am in torments, in insufferable torments."

By this parable Jesus is repeating the same lesson. Only, this time he hits the coast regions with more tenderness. When he made the investigating faculty of man scream and twist itself fast to exhibit what it is at, he let himself in full swing. The whole coast region was afraid of him. The inhabitants urged him to depart out of their coasts in spite of the wonderful healing powers he had shown. By today's parable he exhibits nothing on the coasts but tells that wonderful blessings belong there.

He says, practically, that all investigations are fruitless. They do not come out anywhere. Even telegraphing and telephoning, Pullman sleepers, and dental parlors; X-rays and Wall Street, have not made the multitudes any more joyous. All these things have filled up a few gold pockets, fed a few million with opportunities to chop wood and

black boots, but the joy principle they have un-
touched.

But said the Master Man of the ages, let both
faculties of man be employed by repentance and
the angels will sing so the earth can hear them,
the earth will sing so the heavens can hear it. Angels are the kind thoughts of man, out searching
for a peaceable home. Angels are the beauty concepts of man, out hunting for a realm of smiles.
Angels are the religious thoughts of man on the
wing after a happy land. Angels are the wisdom
calculations of man, as mathematics and gram-
matical constructions, out searching for perfection.
Not one of them has ever been happy, according to
the best records, for everyone has mourned so over
the miseries of the people of this world that it
couldn't be at rest anywhere.

But by repentance, or turning to speak to the
mysterious one behind him, man will find exactly
what he has projected himself forward to get. Man
can bring the sun of God behind him, to shine on
his world ahead of him, by first finding that sun.
And this is the Jesus Christ character manifest on
the coasts again. When, Jesus the man whose eyes
were watching God, went out of the coasts of
Gadara, at the request of the mob, and off the
planet also at the request of the mob, nobody ever
after found any of the principles of Jesus Christ in
his business affairs or in his body. Body has been a
very troublesome thing; business affairs have wor-

ried, family life has tired. The coast regions have been destitute of the ways of Jesus Christ.

It is not likely that anybody but a Christ-like equality of man would discover that the birds have a divine quality.

Pulpit preachers tell us, and must, that we are doing it to please God. They teach that we must be dreadfully sorry that we have ever done any other way at all. They show us that we must cry and wail over our past and loss till we feel the peace of having cried enough. This they call forgiveness.

The church of India and Tibet, the constant instructors of the still and hopeless type declare that if we want to get the Father, divine self, we must go through quite a set of exercises.

Repentance Among the Orientals

The Bhagavad Gita is the instruction book of the orient. If we want to know their formula for repentance or turning from the old and finding God in us, practice their high styles of operation. The following is the first thereof:

"Having placed in a clean spot one's seat firm, not very high nor very low, and a deerskin placed upon a cloth and kusa grass then holding the body, neck, and head straight and unmoved, perfection is determined, and as if beholding the end of his own nose, and not looking in any direction, etc."

This continued, among us as we live, may possibly do something within us, but they doubt hold (sentence is missing here due to tape, which is dark) during this incarnation of ourselves.

Neither the eastern half nor the western half of this globe claims that joy is not possible right here, now, by what can happen when we are here on this round of existence practicing their exercises. Joy is known as a conduct of steady repentance by either set. But Jesus taught that joy is a contagion from the Father when we really repent. He knew both sides of repentance, as practiced by those of the earth during his visible visit. He said the only difference from the way that would strike the chords of joy consisted in projecting themselves forward while the Father House lies behind, while it is the Father's place to attend to what lies around us and beyond us.

It is called in this parable a younger practice to wail over our past and begin to feed the poorhouse people; and so it really is. Feel the consideration of our neighbors without any interest to give them some help is often thought to be a young spendthrift habit both to mind and money by the elder religions. But it seems, in all the parables of Jesus, if it were the one who practiced everything as heard tell of, as hard as ever he could that finally hit the right repentance. Only such a one could begin such a hitherto unpracticed performance as purposely reaching with all his energies backward toward the place where he first called home. Only such a One could be so seemingly negligent as to think it is possible that among the man-blooms of the cycles one might have lived who knew much of the Father that he was Father and who by knowing the name of the Father in its unspeakable power, might charge his own name with opening glory as of gates into somewhere. Who, by taking all the experiences of this earth, set man free from being obliged to go through them; who by ascending unto the Father on the beaming light of his own soul could draw all the sun of the world unto him.

In verse 21 the son begins to tell about his unsuccessful projecting of himself for and over mathematics, politics, religion, ethics, business, pleasure, etc., but the father does not notice this lingo. He immediately clothes him in beauty, feeds him in plenty, showers him in light, and the son forgets his former self at once. He is like a rose in the garden of night, over which the morning sun shines, just as it has been calling itself a homely, unprofitable, unbeautiful rose, deny it smells its own fragrance. Suddenly it laughs on the gleaming day with the endless of unprecedented, unprophesied joy.

According to this lesson, the activity of our being shall exercise itself in calling toward the one who sent us on this journey whose throne place is behind us. And this brings joy. And our joy is contagious now for many people there are who read and talk, drive, and study to divert their minds on their environments. But does it prove effectual as a joy bringing exercise? Does the face laugh with contagious enchantment? Jesus, in this chapter, declares that joy is the birthright of every man, woman, and child.

The angels can never be joyous while mankind weep; while even one of the cashiers in a store is tired. The high flight of scientific men drives them, but they cannot have contagious joy there to beam around them. They are bored out of their wits by even their families if those facilities do not know about acids, equinoxes, molecules, or Greek rocks.

Somewhere there was an academy over the door of which was written: "He that has not learned, let him not enter here." But over Jesus' door it reads: "I am the light of the world." Over the door of our neighbor reads: "He that is not ready rich cannot come in here." But over Jesus does it reads: "Whosoever will, let him come."

These un-shining rays of using the given faculty which each of us possesses are rays of the world. The Christ-like way of turning and calling is the using of our sun on our life. There is a sun that pulls on the mind as there is a sun that pulls on the rose of a garden. As the mind turns toward the sun it sees itself in a new light. It is even said that it is not of the nature of mind any longer when it feels that sun.

If mind finds itself all illuminated with beauty so permeating that every molecule of the body is beautiful with it, it is in the sun. If mind finds itself all alive with the knowing all things so quickeningly that the tongue cannot speak except with wonderful words far-spreading joy, then it is in the sun. If mind finds itself tasting of a lesser kind of experience, so glad in its kind that miracles arrive in the home without being worked for, then it is in the sun. If one knows without thinking, and believes one works without working itself into anyone then it is not mind, but is the original one. "In such an hour as ye think not the sun cometh."

The sun that is so competent is who this lesson calls "The Father." No matter where the mind went, or where it stayed, it was grumbling and lamenting till it got into the sun. And the sun, the Father, was always on the home spot. Jove is always on this throne. The I Am always has enough exchange for a world of husks. The sun is always in authority. The Father, Sun, always shines on any body who turns in his joy. "Joy" is the mysterious name of the mysterious Father's influence. "Joy" is the force by which the pulling beams of the shining sun of this age are mentioned by Jesus in Perea, January A.D. 30. And unless this joy is of some untold new person it says plainly that even the angels are transformed by it.

Now, that the repentance Jesus actually preached has not heretofore been taught plain enough; for this lesson makes it that with the real act of repentance there was a quick instantaneous, and immediate supply of everything from the mental interior state to the outer or coast state where the common doing of human life go to any man who lacks any thing or if in trouble of any sort, he has never repented though as pious as a kemper (one who strives or contends).

The Inter Ocean Newspaper, April 19, 1896

Lesson IV

Out Of The Range Of Mind

Luke 16:19-31

Luke recorded certain parables which no other New Testament writers remembered to put down, today's lesson is one of them. Luke addressed his book to Theophilius; not a man but the divinity spark in all men. Luke was an idealist, a healer, an artist, a mystic. He wrote up these Perean parables as an idealist.

Today's lesson was given near Bethabara in the Perean pilgrimage. Bethabara means "fording place." That is in ideality, the place where we cross from mind to the mindless. From idea to the meta-idea. Meta means above, out of the range of matter? If there is something out of the range of matter, is there not something out of the range of mind?

We might hack away to our children for another ten years on the same old lines of explanation which religious books have been giving to these parables for hundreds of years, but there are some other meanings which are far more efficient in execution with character. For we now find that there is a way of writing that can subtly undermine all the former mind and all the old character, and even turn the body and business upside down and set them up again to correspond with itself.

These Inter-Ocean lessons are built for that undermining and reconstructing purpose. People are beginning to notice that even the bluest relig-ions papers and preachers are unguardedly altering a few of their first positions into these lines, though they have been so violently opposed to these transcendental ways of understanding the wonderful Jesus that they have said at times that they were dangerous reading matter.

Lessons Are Doing Good

They are, probably not aware how they are floundering around trying to catch at the old straws of their former teachings. But these lessons are truly operating on their mentals in an irre-sistible fashion. So, in one sense, some of those pious men who called these writings dangerous to life and limb were right, for they are subtly and secretly causing old things to touch quicksand.

As all readers of these lessons have been duly warned that they are capable of laying hold of the thoughts of the mind, as well as the limbs and bank stock of human transactions, they have been voluntarily taking their lives into their own hands by reading them.

Today's lesson is more dangerous than any of the preceding ones, for it takes us right into heaven and there exposes how the people's minds, which they kept secret on this earth, are made as plain as daylight.

Dives had a secret mind, while he was eating humming bird's heads and perfuming his beard as an inhabitant of this earth. Lazarus also had a secret mind while the sores were running on his body and his stomach was famishing, during his acquaintance with Dives in the capacity of pauper and capitalist on this earth. These secret minds broke loose on creation, in both cases, after burial of their material bodies. Dives used to make hast to talk and laugh with his comrades, so that outside he should not get the horrors. He, doubtless, was a great scholar of some sort, for nothing diverts the outer mind from the inner ideal like good company end a thorough knowledge of some science.

Lazarus and Dives

Lazarus was obliged to divert his outer mind from outer miseries by studying into the inner sanctuary of his hidden ideals, for nothing diverts the outer mind from pain like contemplation of the secret ideal spot common to all humanity. Dives was on the same tack as Lazarus, but not on the same track. If Lazarus had had Dives' opportunities for diverting his outer mind by eating and

study, doubtless he, too, would have got into ha-
des. Not many people, with good external chances
to divert their outer mind away from itself ever
look deeply into the hidden Perea.

"But this lesson is about people with good
chances to divert and with poor chances to divert.
There are theaters, operas, cathedrals, clubs, for
Dives, but only dogs, crying hunger, rags, for
Lazarus.

Now, pleasure is a diversion of outer mind,
away from ideals, and away from itself. Pain is a
diversion of outer mind toward a getting away out
of what we are caught into. "Take me out! Help
me!" is its cry. This shows that it is looking to a
free spot — a Perea. Pleasure yells, "Let me stay
here always!" Pain causes the outer mind to seek
for the help so desperately that it finally hits the
ideal spot within. For, there is never anybody to
help a Lazarus on the outer plane. He is Job. Did
anybody help Job? In order to be a regular Lazarus, you must have people talk metaphysics to
you, when it is the unspeakable you want, with its
competence to attend to your life. The metaphysi-
cian explains how you are to blame for your
trouble. Thoughts have made you miserable. The
material doctor says you have eaten too much
slops or too little slops. But neither one can help
you if you are an out and out Lazarus. You must
be mentally and physically starved, and mentally
and physically in pain in order to be a regular
Lazarus man. Never mind what made you a Laza-

rus, never mind what made you a Dives. Never mind about your Karma. Take yourself where you stand. How are you diverting yourself?

Death Is Not an End

Death, so called, does not stop your career. It does not stop your character. It simply shows up the fruits of your earthly diversions of your outer mind. If, away from the Perea spot, the ideal within, then how can you expect to go through that gate into the realm beyond the ideal?

It was by repeating over the formulas given us by people who had looked into the ideal that we found their divinest descriptions were incompetent. When description of beauty is incompetent to describe what we see, we are near the unspeakable. We are at the ford, Bethabara. At the place in mind which this lesson describes objectively.

Notice, Dives had carried along his domineering mind. He began to order the old patriarch Abraham around, even after he had disposed of his flesh. (Luke 16:19-51) He still spoke of Lazarus as a scullion and a donkey. (Verse 24)

But Lazarus had not taken even the slightest notice of Dives. Indeed, Abraham told Dives that there was such a gulf between the idealist's conditions, after death, and the materialist's that Lazarus could not possibly remember how it had ever seemed to him to be subject to material things. (Verse 26)

Luke is an idealist from beginning to end. He takes the lesson of Jesus on this subject of the fruitage of diversion, and talks of Dives and Lazarus, who are not men but states. All commentators agree that "Dives" means rich worldly opportunities for turning the mind to please the senses, and "Lazarus" means poor worldly chances for the same. They can't see at all, though, that "Theophilius" is used figuratively also.

Notice that Jesus at the ford on earth talks of the "gulf" in the other world. One has to cross the gulf from diverting the mind with material and intellectual pleasures here into noticing the lofty statements of soul equality and divine influences, or he will see the same old gulf staring him in the face on the other side, with an intensity of difference.

"As the tree falls so it lies." As the people think here, so they catch the fruits there. Some fruits come ripe here; but the great matter of how we divert our minds is settled best there.

Abraham's Double Vision

Abraham can see both states. His very name shows that he is the watch- guard over fidelity. Dives has been faithful to his style of life, he worked at it every day. (Verse 19) Lazarus had been faithful to his practice of adoring his silent descriptions of the delights of free peace, free health, free leave of the earth. Neither one had any description of settling accounts here in this state of mind called earth.

The very fact that Dives is always afraid to be alone shows he likes the outer diversions his chances give him. The very fact that Lazarus likes to be alone with his ideals shows he does not like his outer chances. Probably at one time, while he was at the gates of praise, thinking of the ravishing joys laid up for the people of God, he had detected that his outer environments were on this earth, the fruits of his own thoughts. They were his graven images against the indescribable splendor of the presence of God. If he did discover that, he asked to be forgiven for thinking anything at all. At the point of being forgiven for thinking such thoughts as would make a material environment, he touched the chord that awoke his eyes to see an ethereal environment.

All existence or showing forth is product of thinking. All thinking is determined to picture itself somehow. Thus, in having something given for our thinking, which, as these past lessons have taught is forgiveness, we must have surroundings somewhere which are thrown around us by the thinkless One.

(On the manuscript the first line was cut away) own I Am, which is one with the holy I Am.

What Moses Taught

Moses, the great thinker of noble proclamations, touched moments at the ford between thinking and not thinking. "Thou shalt not make unto thee any graven image, he said. He said also: "The Lord shall fight for you, and you shall hold your peace." We cannot be peaceable while we think anything at all. We cannot stop thinking until we have been forgiven for thinking. We must have forgiveness for existence, or graven images everywhere, as Schopenhauer, Plato, Lakya Muni, and thousands of others have found that we do. "The world is my own mental picture," they say.

Then we must be forgiven for thinking, speaking, writing, working, all of which exercises make pictures. They all surround us with environments of our own make, and a mighty poor lot we make. So, the secret purport of this lesson is that we had better strike forgiveness right now, though there is no doubt we can get it after we have laid down the material body, which we have formulated by thought, speech, writings, workings. "If I make my bed in hell, thou art there," sang David. He knew that a man makes his own hell.

> "I sent my soul out through the universe,
>   Some letter of the after life to spell;
> And by and by my soul returned to me
>   And answered, "1 myself am heaven or hell,"

The thinkless one at our headquarters has a country, or kingdom, or realm, whatever we may choose to name it. They who are forgiven for thinking are suddenly ushered into view of it. This lesson does not say that Lazarus had got sight of it, though his oblivion to all that Dives said and felt would intimate that he had been forgiven for thinking, speaking, writing, working.

He does not even hear Dives speaking of him as a minion. And Dives cannot stop thinking that Lazarus is still a serf. He cannot ask Abraham for the privilege of going back and doing his own preaching. He had always had his own way of working by ordering, tongue fashion, just what he wanted done, and ordering punishments for slight offenses, also by tongue. This same habit pursued him, intensified so far that he could not catch his wits enough to think of going back to his five brothers and telling them how to change their minds.

All Science Is Immature

All science of mind which has formulas for right thoughts is excellent, but it is science in the green. All science of mind which has the injunction to do works is excellent, but it is science in the green. The Christian science of our country has works, works, works, for its cry. Schlatter was a picture formed in space by the continual harping on "works" by Christian scientists. The Swami was a picture formed in space by the continual harping on "words" kept up by another set who changed their names both personal and general, sometimes calling them selves mentalists, sometimes meta-physicians, sometimes Christians.

Even their names, as Thomas, Mary, John, or Ann, they turned into spiritual meanings and harped on those.

The Swami seemed to do nothing but talk. Schlatter seemed to do nothing but work. Neither one had crossed the Bethabara ford here. They both give evidences of crossing it on Abraham's bosom in the next world. The Jesus Christ teaching at its sweetest touch is neither Swami nor Schlatter. "Behold, I make." "In such an hour as ye think not." "They rest from their labors and their works do follow them."

All science is a preparation to get rid of the evil which may possibly lie ahead of us. Did not Jesus tell us to stop trying to protect ourselves in advance? "Let the morrow take care for the things of itself." "Take no thought for the marrow." Did he not say that this very day itself is competent to arrange its own evil affairs without our meddling? "Sufficient unto the day is the evil thereof." Just as if all evil, even our deafness and lameness, were to be thrown off onto the day itself. That mysterious ether that now surrounds us filling all the air with pictures of our own minds.

Some Important Lessons

What a mighty lesson this Luke lesson of Dives and Lazarus is! Lazarus forgiven for thinking; Dives determined to think. Lazarus crossed from describing God by religious axioms to letting God attend to his own business. Dives not stopping from anything an instant to let be what is. Neither one catching the product till he laid off his earth body.

Let other ways of explaining this text keep on with the same old dogmatics and let the same old environments swing their pictures around those who hang on to them. Let this fact be known, however, that, now that another reading of them has touched the hidden spring in somebody, somewhere there must another set of conditions become visible.

If we keep up the same interpretations we shall see the same world. If we interpret differently we shall see another world. If we interpret nothing, but let the divine fact show on the empyrean walls of the glorious majesty enfolding us just what it pleases, we are forgiven for interpretation. Why should we leave our Father's house to go out telling anything? Cannot our Father print his own country on our circumambient airs?

Who is willing to be forgiven for existing? Who loves the world he has made by graving thoughts on space so well that he will stick to it faithfully, like Dives? Who is so interested in what is going on around him that he still feels that he must go to and fro, either with words or works, meddling and dickering with his own world? Such a one knows not Jesus at the ford spot, Bethabara of Perea: The matchless day of letting the divine will be done.

Inter Ocean Newspaper, April 26, 1896

(Dives and Lazarus or Lazarus and Dives is a narrative attributed to Jesus that is reported only in the Gospel of Luke (Luke 16:19-31). It is also known as "The Rich Man and the Beggar Lazarus." In the Vulgate Biblical text, since the rich man is not named, he is referred to as Dives from dives, the Latin word for rich man. The story has been a favourite for artists and theologians, as it is the most vivid account of an afterlife to be found in the New Testament.)

LESSON V

Going Toward Jerusalem

Luke 17:5-10

The golden text of this lesson serves for the key idea of a week's experiences. It is a certain request made by the early Christian ministers of Jesus Christ — "Lord, increase our faith." They did not tell him what they wanted to put their faith into, but they urged him to give them a treatment to bring up their hidden faith nature.

It is likely that they knew that if that faith nature could get to bubbling up and boiling over they could charge up any sort of object with energy, and make it do things. A pianist gets his fingers so nimble by training them that they can obey the eyesight faster than the eyes could possibly chase them around. There have been conjurors who have detected that their balls and cups were acting like skillful creatures after long drills with the same performances.

A clover leaf will cure you of deafness if you will train it to that business. The invisible force that is forever hanging around this mundane sphere will do anything you charge it up to do after you have dinged at it long enough. It takes only a tiny bit of actual confidence in a stick of wood or an invisible deity to make it perform very good healing of sickness and readjustment of affairs.

Take notice, you yourself have to work at these things, whether gods or stones, with some quality or faculty already inherent within yourself before they will do anything at all.

Therefore the working principle is your inherent nature, drawn forth by some sort of practice. In this lesson Jesus is requested by the apostles to pound on them or massage them, either by his thoughts or his fingers to hurry their sluggish faith nature into useful prominence. He says that heretofore they have been feeding up and massaging their servants, and did not know it. (Luke 17:5-10)

God is Always a Helper

"Do you not know that it is the actual business of this universe to wait on you, provide for you, make you supremely happy and illuminate you with wisdom?" he asks. "Did you think it was your business to make the mighty God do things for you by coaxing, tears, or praises? Through the grass and through the cosmic dusts, I tell you, the same serving energy waits and smiles. It is your privilege to command your need, not beg or flatter any-thing anymore." (Verses 7, 8, 9, 10)

In the tenth verse he adds: "This is the least of your prerogatives. Ye are very small nobodies if ye have got no farther in the use of your own inherent grandeurs than to know how to charge up your hands or your tongues or eyeballs with healing gases."

In the eleventh verse he says that the whole splendor of achievement consists in going toward Jerusalem, or the "I Am" of ourselves. He shows that as we rise up to be what we are we go through Samaria and Galilee. That is, we find ourselves protected from the arrows of hurt that are slung against us, and we find ourselves taken out of some state of affairs by a miracle. This did not require our faith. It did itself. Jesus preached no faith in God as necessary to God's good dealings with us, though he often praised people for pour-ing so much of their faith into himself, not because he would do any more for the world by reason of it, but because the reaction would be so good for themselves.

For they would touch something alive, and feel its life when they touched him with their confi-dence. He often praised a great faith as nowadays we praise great muscles or great riches. He knew what an irresistible thing it is, and that things have to spin and twist to obey its lightest words.

Must be Prepared by Faith

In the verses where it tells of his meeting ten lepers, and only one had any responsive life in himself, he made a practical illustration of things as they run. Some things have a more trained state already, when we touch them, than others. Somebody has worked over them with their faith more or less, and they respond better when we touch them with our faith. We really put our quantum of faith with what was already put there by some predecessor, and it comes near making a grain.

He took ten lepers. They were the least promising specimens of responsiveness he could call up. The Sunday-school books will tell you what poor stuff they are. One of these had had something touch near his well of conviction at some past date. So he felt the quickening from within, as well as from without, when Jesus touched him.

The rest were emblems of the clover leaves and quinine pills of daily medication. They cure while the doctors stick to them, and won't do a thing when they let them alone.

A few years ago doctors bled everybody for everything that ailed them. And it worked well. But on a day there arose some doctors who would not believe in blood-letting. Then it wouldn't' help anybody. The powdered thigh bone of a criminal was formerly a great remedy. It was a "leper" that had never been touched at its quickening point. So

after a while powdered thigh bones would not
work.

Men Refuse Assistance

Nine things out of ten have not been trained to
do anything on their own account. This is what
this lesson of Jesus means. The whole creation
refuses to do anything at all till it is prodded up.
This is what ten lepers mean. All things have their
God pivot. Find it. One thing out of ten will easily
show it forth. But the main point is to be putting
for or toward your own pivotal energy. Then you
can detect what is already near breaking open,
and what needs a great deal of pounding. This is
what "going toward Jerusalem" means.

Any other meaning is tiresome and has no
more startling good in it than the present state of
civilization. Does anybody think the world has
arrived anywhere simply because we have factories builded and run by men who were compelled
to build and run them or starve? Does anybody
think the world has arrived anywhere just because
we have newspapers and telegraphs that can
quickly report murders and arsons? Yet these
things are the products of the kind of understanding of Jesus which his followers have been giving
us for more than a thousand years.

Every kind or degree of understanding does its
own mission with mankind. Keep your eyes open
for the fruitage of this new kind of understanding
of the gospel of Jesus Christ.

Take notice that it is the understanding of a thing that handles it. And it won't serve you unless you understand it. But what is that understanding which is so important to have in order to move things to suit you? Is it not something that springs up from within yourself? Now Jesus was the one only object and subject that has arrived on this planet who asked no faith in himself and no understanding of him in order to be something supernal and do mighty works. "If I do not the works of the father, believe me not," he said. Did he not mean that he would do and be something first before ever mankind would have to have faith in him?

Jesus Alone Was Perfect

He was the one thing that has come hither preferring to be Immaculate of man's faith and man's understanding. He was neither a clover leaf, a poultice, nor a deity needing to be set going by somebody's faith. He stood alone and was what he was on his own account. As his Father had life in himself, so he also had life in himself. The self derivative nature of man was a great theme with Jesus. How he derives his faith from his own self. How he derives his understanding from his own self. How he protects and guides his life from within his own self. He must be forever headed toward Jerusalem, his own inexhaustible self.

Jesus taught that Jerusalem does not need any faith or understanding. Jerusalem is the name that means Father-God, Mother-God, Son-God. In this wonderful substance is all that we can use or mention, besides much more that is unspeakable, and all the native inheritance of mankind without his having to exercise faith or understanding.

The obligation to have faith in a pill before it will operate is a heavy burden. The obligation to have faith in a formula before it will do anything is a heavy burden. The obligation to understand anything before it will serve you is a heavy burden. The obligation to understand or have faith in Jesus before he will work is a heavy burden.

An Important Lesson

Therefore, Jesus taught this lesson of heading for Jerusalem and letting it take care of you as a more divinely kind way of life than working for malt extracts, formulae, and deities great or small by dragging on the faith nature.

Even if you get a deity so he will move mountains you have achieved nothing, he said. (Verse 10) It was your duty to bring up faith and move the mountains while you were in the mountain business, he said. But when you are out of the mountain business you will find the original energy which will not ask your assistance to smooth out the wrinkles of trial.

Galilee means close of a dispensation; it is a wonderful rest to close a dispensation. The principle dispensation to close is the hard doctrine of faith. Have faith, have faith, have faith, we are told.

The very Christian science that rose like a vapory perfume out of the rocky terrors of Calvinism declared that some people could use its formulas effectively and some couldn't.

Some could sit and think about how unreal your eyeballs were and by that meditation make your eyesight good, while others might sit and think that doctrine forty years and it would not work. Everything required such impossible and extraordinary conditions to make it good for anything. Even God himself would not stir for some faithful hearts, but would work like a cyclone for some hardhearted bigots. (Verse 17)

All Hope Is In the Lord

Jesus knew about this and eased up on mankind by showing them himself as one with Jerusalem. And neither he as Jerusalem, nor Jerusalem as he, needed any confidence put into them. What a restful lesson this is. We need not even prod ourselves up with self-confidence. Like Esther when she faced Xerxes, without faith in anybody or anything, yet the greatest of armies could hardly have accomplished more. Lo, whether we be good or bad, small or great, poor or rich, counts for nothing. Whether we have faith or doubt, whether we can recite scripture or not, whether we can praise or curse best, counts for nothing.

The pivotal city around which we are swinging is immaculate of such things as we can offer. So we offer nothing. But we turn that way. We take notice of our Jerusalem. We know that it is the divine giver of all things. Jesus was the bloom of centuries of search after God, the merciful provider. He touched that God. Then he showed man how to charge up rocks with healing powers, also deities and scripture verses. Then he showed that such charging up was not what he came to declare. He came to declare something that asks none of our energies. It asks nothing. Prefers that we should offer it nothing. Says often: "Rest in the Lord and he shall bring it to pass." The Lord is another name for Jerusalem. And Jerusalem is a strange name of the pivotal center of divine power. Jesus took the name of the soul. Then he took his own name. Soul is also a strange name for the center of divine power. It has so many names because it has no name which the tongue of man can speak, or his mind think.

The End of the Dispensation

It is high noon with the body when it sitteth down to stop struggling with things to make them work. It is high noon with mind when it keepeth itself quiet after having recited formulas and axioms and texts by the yard. Solomon sang to his own soul: "Where markest thou thy flocks to rest at noon?" So then, they who know that even their faith may now rest, are striking toward the end of the world. Toward the end of dispensation. The soul maketh its flocks to rest from faith, from love, from understanding. As Jesus stood on the soul point of himself he had the soul name. This made

him as obedient as soul. Nothing obeys like the
soul, the Jerusalem. It does everything we command. Nothing else is so obedient. Nothing so
profoundly a servant to "He that is greatest among
you let him be your servant." So the greatest servant is he who requires least faith and friendship
of his master. Therefore, the soul is the greatest
servant, for it requires neither praise nor blame,
neither faith nor doubt, neither friendship nor
enmity, to do all the works we can command to be
done.

The Soul is a Mystery
The soul of man is a mystery. It is that which
setteth man's house in order at his command, yet
is something that knoweth nothing about order. It
is the unexplainable. We may tell how they make
lightning in the laboratory, but not one can tell
how the soul, being so almighty, is yet the profoundly obedient. Nor how the soul dealing like a
rich city with man yet knows neither of man nor
his wants, forever must external man be a
stranger to the wonderful soul. (Verse 18) Though,
at his highest gladness in soul, yet a stranger. The
moment he touches the soul he is not visible to
external man. The moment he enters Jerusalem
he disappears. This lesson declares that faith in
man is excellent while he is dealing with external
affairs for the purpose of making them do something. It declares that to return and praise the
soul is good also. It is brightening to life to praise
the Lord. It also declares that God, whose name is

Soul, whose name is 'I Am', whose name is Lord, whose name is Jesus Christ, is not reached by praises. This was the last month of the external march of Jesus toward Jerusalem to symbolize his silent gaze on the New Jerusalem. At the outer Jerusalem he was crucified to symbolize the end of his use of faith, love, and understanding. These qualities are not needed at the point where the New Jerusalem is entered. That city has its rest for those who have exercised those virtues. To the outer man, Jesus seemed to die at Jerusalem. To himself he was self-forgiven for having built a world of human beings by thoughts and for having had a mind of love and faith.

This lesson teaches that in a profoundly sweet sense man must touch the point of being forgiven for ever having had faith in anybody or anything — even in the absolute and eternal Deity himself. Last Sunday's lesson set this forth most clearly. It properly matches this one of today. They all go in pairs.

Inter Ocean Newspaper, May 3, 1896

LESSON VI

The Publican And The Pharisee

Luke 18:9-17

"Glory is like a circle in the water,
Which never ceaseth to enlarge itself,
Till by broad spreading it dispersed to naught."

"Die and live again! For so long as thou hast not
done so thou art naught but a bewildered stranger
upon a darksome earth."

Today's Bible Lesson gives the Perean doctrine
of repentance. The Perean doctrine of anything
must be the most radical that the parable will
permit.

It must step beyond the bounds of the ordinary. The publican of this chapter represents the
principle of repentance from the thoughts of evil
and pain as powers. That is easy. The Pharisee
represents the principle of repentance from the
thoughts of good as a power. That is hard. The
first part of repentance is turning half way round

59

toward Him on the throne. The second part of repentance is turning the other half of the way around. Something changes with every step of the turn. This is forgiveness.

The environment that closes around you now is your existence. You made it look as it does by your sense of it. Truly in its actual it is quite different from your sense of it. To get the eyes and ears lighted by the flame of the Eternal One is to get an entirely different sense. This is forgiveness for existence.

To stop the present sense is the Jesus Christ death. "I am he that liveth and was dead." It was death, or end of the sense of things as He found it reigning, that Jesus of Nazareth published. He proclaimed it at its second turn, where man thinks that good deeds and good thoughts are great things, a harder task than at its first turn, where man thinks that cruel deeds are a part of the scheme of creation.

To stop making thoughts that make up a fictitious environment and then to have a truer sense of the kingdom around us, is forgiveness for existence. To stop having faith in people, things, or God himself, is to have a better view of the Actual. This is forgiveness for having had faith. To stop doing good works, such as clothing, feeding, healing, teaching, preaching, is to have a sight of people and animals and plants in their actual state. This is forgiveness for good words and good works. This is today's subject.

A hypnotist can change his neighbor's sense of an orange or an eyeball so that to him there may be sight of nothing or sight of something. The performances of the adepts of the Orient are hypnotic influences on large scales. That is, changing the sense of things in a whole crowd simultaneously. This is imitation of forgiveness. They give another sense of things for the old sense.

Jesus knew the hypnotized state of mankind, wherein they were always seeing pain and pleasure, beauty and horribleness, riches and poverty, male and female. He knew that the sense with which mankind were seeing these contrasts ought to stop and let mankind see things as they really are. He saw that to atop our sense of things could only be done by repentance, that is, a sudden turning to see who is just behind us and how He regards things. "Thou shalt hear a voice behind thee saying, This is the way, walk ye in it." This turning cuts off the external objective world. And this is death. "He that would save his life must lose it." Then, by some mighty miracle, the eyesight gets lighted at the altar fires of the One forever behind us, and we discover ourselves feeling differently about our environments.

The Panorama of Life Is Forgiveness
The One behind is sometimes called 'The Lamb," because it, or he, or she turns out to be such a neutral to existence, such a dissolver of existence, such a transformer of existence. The

new set of panoramas that begins to turn itself around our life is forgiveness.

We are to have forgiveness for having a world of opposite conditions whirling itself around us. We have no business to have the sick on one hand, the well on another, the deformed in plain sight, and the beautiful flaunting its contrasts close to it.

We have no business with kind thoughts on our right hand and hateful anathemas on our left hand, toppling us into misery tomorrow after we had been in such ecstasy yesterday. There is a power behind us, a force, a wonder, a Nameless One who never sees these opposites, because He is not hypnotized.

This un-hypnotized One is called "He" in all Bibles, by spells, then "She", then "It". These different genders are applied because no gender belongs to the Wonderful One. This un-hypnotized glory just behind us is often called "Lord" often called "God," often called "Soul", often called "Spirit", once called "Ruth", lastly called "Jesus Christ".

These different names are applied because the actual name is not given till the actual forgiveness has taken place. "I will give him a new name which no man can read, saving he that receiveth it."

Last Sunday's Lesson showed that this Wonderful One does not ask us to have any faith in Him at all. That lesson showed that Jesus did not demand faiths He even showed that it involved people deeper into hypnotism then anything else.

Today's lesson shows us that faith lands us into a state where we do not have strength to turn toward the Voice just behind. So cannot even think there is such a voice. "John the Revelator made a violent wrench to get himself out of the clutches of his faith, love, and goodness."

"I turned to see the voice," he said. It sounds absurd to the present hypnotized man to talk of seeing a voice, but in the state of the Wonderful One there is no distinction between hearing and seeing. Those two pompous liars are quite dead, and there is no memory of their several offices for him that turneth to behold the voice.

Today's lesson teaches that man shall have forgiveness for his goodness equally as for his badness. Its text may be found in Luke 18:9-17. You will see that the man in goodness, love, mercy, truth, has tougher knot to loose than the man in badness. Did you ever see the glorious face of a martyr for the "truth" while he was accusing you of some misdemeanor you were not guilty of? How inflexible the smelted steal of his face, the unquenchable fire of his eyes! Nothing could shake his determination to punish you for his sense of you.

A Christian of the Regular Church

Today's lesson brings up that good punisher of evil so honored by church and state, and shown that he needs forgiveness for being good, truthful, trusting, generous, chaste, kind, upright, merciful. It shows plainly that whoever practices all these virtues is in a state where he sees wickedness on one hand and goodness on another. He is a Christian of the regular church.

This lesson shows how one who sees all badness in himself always wants to see the other side of the balances. This turns his vision half way around, and he gets goodness. It is at the point of conscious goodness in ourselves with the badness plainly outside of ourselves, that we stick. This takes in the saints of earth, all who punish evil or try to shun evil. To the final repentant one there is neither good nor evil. He has repented of having been good. Good is the balance of evil.

Beauty is the balance of ugliness. One never gets the advantage of the other, but each recruits its ranks from the other as much and as often as necessary to keep the balance equal. So our ministers and teachers never get ahead a peg. They only haul what they call sin over into what they call holiness, and they get salaries for their efforts. But they are not practicing Jesus Christ, and let them not flatter themselves into supposing that they are. They are only performing the Pharisee act on the balance pole of poverty and riches, goodness and badness. According to this lesson they must repent of trying to convert their neighbors from naughtiness into uprightness.

Of course they will call this interpretation altogether wrong. They will still stick to it that theirs is right. This is seeing their own "rightness" and my "wrongness". They should read over and over the self-treatment of John the Revelator. "I turned to see the voice." "I turned to see the voice." This will pry them slightly up toward repentance. They will, by the influence of John's treatment, cease from trying to convert their neighbors.

They will see Him that sitteth on the throne. The radiant streams that beam from the eternal throne will make these clergymen, missionaries, and philanthropists give forth sweet influences all magical with charm to turn other men toward the wonderful One just behind them. But they can never be these influences while they are standing up for righteousness and punishing evil-doers, or trying to convert their neighbors from error.

During the converting stage of man he is busy more or less with thinking himself in the right, and his neighbors in the wrong. Therefore, during that stage he knows nothing of repentance, remission, or forgiveness.

Righteousness Which Is As Filthy Rags
Ezekiel had a revelation of this same fact nearly 600 B.C. He said that there would come a wind of good that would bind up the broken and strengthen that which was sick, but would destroy the fat and the strong. Binding and strengthening are half forgiveness. Something is waiting to atop these and give in their places.

The Pharisee is anybody who preaches good as the power we ought to serve, or who tells that evil has no power. He must have some kind of a treatment from somewhere that will turn him one more half way round toward the mighty One behind him. At the last swing of man on his pivotal turn toward his starting point he does not discern between goodness and badness.

He is not interested in crime enough to preach against it or punish it. He is not interested in holiness enough to urge it. He is whatever his original wonderfulness makes him to be, and he tries to do and to be nothing else. This is truly what is meant by the fat and the strong being destroyed.

It does not make any difference if we have preached the omnipresence of good and the non-presence of evil till we are shaking with one-sided palsiness and are gray-headed with over-zeal; it is not the final Jesus Christ meaning and we are not radiating our actual possibilities, nor seeing the Kingdom that surrounds us while we are preaching that way. We have another swing to make to unclothe ourselves of the highest, grandest, sweetest righteousness we have ever preached or reached; for all your righteousness is filthy rags, saith the Lord, yea, even all you can reach of loving kindness is naught.

One righteousness that is filthy rags is preaching about goodness. Let us find forgiveness for that operation. Another righteousness that is filthy rags is working for the good of our fellow men. Let us find forgiveness for that operation.

These two righteous rags have had their existence, or outward formulation, manifestation, exhibition, or whatever you please to call it, in two distinctly plain types passing before our eyes lately.

First, the Oriental Swami, who did nothing but talk; second, the Occidental Schlatter, who did nothing but work.

These both did purposely and consciously try to accomplish some good. And they both recruited from the left wing of the balance pole to the right wing of the same. But neither one touched the Jesus Christ ministry. They both need the John treatment for turning to behold the voice. But this lesson declares them to be so satisfied in their way as the right way that they positively will not repent and be forgiven for preaching and working on the side of good health, good strength, good intelligence, good constitution, good looks.

Jesus Christ preached the extinction of both such types as the final result of his voice. You can tell this by the last clause of Verse 14: "He that humbleth himself shall be exalted." Certainly nobody can get humble enough to satisfy the equation till he is extinct.

Symbol of the New Dispensation

The new dispensation is figured, commencing verse 15, by little children. They never claim to know anything or be anything. They never try to be good or bad. They are what they are and the whole household waits on them with servile trembling. Ecstatic if they smile, anguish stricken if they weep. The younger the child the more nearly nothing are its claims and the more nearly frantic the household to please it.

Thus with those who are forgiven for having worded themselves into good raiment like Swami or worked themselves into good fame like Schlatter. Those who turn are great at their throne place. They are nothing in materiality, intellectuality, or possessions; yet, everybody dealing with them catches the radiance of their contiguity with authority and hurries and scurries to serve them, turning all the while away from the glory of cathedrals and factories to the elixirs that wait to make them as little children also. They being forgiven for goodness accomplish the final Jesus Christ ministry.

It is told in astronomy that there are suns shining in our night skies now whose whole existence was long ago blotted out but light travels so slowly that their flames burning so brightly years on years ago have but just arrived here. This lesson of today tells the esoteric student that 1900 years ago Jesus of Nazareth shone on the earth as a morning star with the information that He was forgiven for having created a world of human beings with good and bad proclivities through presuming to cover the actual kingdom with His sense of things.

And in His forgiveness, through His turning away from the glory of doing good, as well as from doing evil, all who were trying to preach good news and practice good conduct might cease from their labors. He stopped the whirring wheels of existence once, not only for himself, but for all mankind. He struck the kingdom of God. He entered it. His name took its whole splendor. Whoever should cease from preaching by word of mouth or writings of pen, and cease from charitable services of humanity, as healing the sick or clothing the naked, on the ground that all this had once been done and forgiven for its doing, should find himself as simple and unpretentious as a little child, yet as radiantly powerful as the kingdom of God. (V erse 17)

This interpretation touches our earth now with apparently no strength, but yet its strength is terrible as an army with banners. For it is the nearer heat of the Jesus Christ meaning that blazed on the stony tablets of a deeply hypnotized humanity 1,900 years ago with the incomprehensible offer: "Come unto me and I will give you rest." That nobody has taken Him at his word in the fiery splendor of its actual meaning comes nothing against its verity. "I am the light of the world" till the end. The morning star of antiquity now flings the hot beams of its prophesied light athwart the thresholds of the many mansions prepared for them that rest in this offer. Cease from the glory of doing good. It is naught. This is the final repentance.

Inter-Ocean Newspaper, May 10, 1896

LESSON VII

The Last Great Week

Luke 19:11-27

The lesson of today, although it is located in Jericho, is in the Perean section and closes it, it opens up what is called "the last great week".

However diverting history of events may be to some people, we must bear in mind that there is something besides diversion wanted by the rest of the world.

So, the story of the travels and talks of Jesus of Nazareth is not at all, not the slightest bit, even, interesting to many, many millions, if it does not have something in it of vital energy for daily life. And, moreover, it must have something different from the usual Sunday-school rendering, which has been going on since Robert Raikes time for young folks and since the early church fathers' time for adults.

Looking back over the International Bible lessons for the last four years as given by these

71

columns of The Inter-Ocean we find that not one of them has stopped to rest on the fence of those time-honored and hard-struggling explanations set forth in the Sunday-school quarterlies used by the rest of the world of Christians. Therefore, their influence is wholly unlike those jading excitants, for they tell the world that the Lord Jehovah is not such a disappointed, grieved, easily angered, revengeful, hard-working, but much-defeated being as the old interpreters have made out.

This then, is a restful influence while the other is a driving force. It is the fulfillment of a prophecy as to the effect of giving the incontrovertible meaning of Jesus Christ. "They rest from their labors and their works do follow them." "These signs shall follow them." Is it not restful to know that our works follow our presence and in no way depend upon its exertions?

The golden text of today is a very good keynote to the meaning of Jesus. "He that is faithful in that which is least is faithful also in much." There is another text that would have been equally its keynote. It is this: "Every idle word that men shall speak they shall give account thereof in the day of judgment." There is still another. It is this: "The poor ye have always with you."

Jericho means fragrant place. Whatever is spoken here has multiplying quality in it. This interpretation that I will now give has in itself the multiplication of some one item for everybody who reads it. Some people are prosperity multiplied;

some are health multiplied; some are intelligence multiplied. Whatever is multiplied we may be certain will be what we will like.

The Fruits of the Spirit Are Light

For the fruits of this spirit are light and life-awakening. There is no punishing, revenging, dread-bringing in them, not even for so-called sinners. Last Sunday's lesson showed that no one man is more sinful than another. They are all alike, each operating on his own plane; and this lesson assures the most unpropitious among them that it will multiply something for him the coming week.

It is the hackneyed story of the ten pounds, generally explained as making the best use of our talents, etc. Taking the Jericho interpretation, it does not mean anything of the kind. (Luke 19:11-27) Jesus, as you may read here (verse 11), was "nigh Jerusalem," Jericho was his stopping place, close to Jerusalem. It stands for a consciousness that now strikes all who have been turning toward their own I AM and reading up that journey of Jesus 1900 years ago, with which he exactly described all the experiences of those who take that journey toward touching the Father at our headquarters. He means by this lesson that there is such a thing as conscious-acquaintance with the all-giving, all-doing God. At the Jericho point we ask what we will, and it is done; or we have it done whether we ask or not. This place is fragrant with wonderful accomplishments in our particular behalf. One of us thought we had only one chance, one opportunity, one possession; but we find it is ten.

One thought that he had but one thing endurable in his life; but he finds suddenly that he has five wonderful movements in his behalf. One is utterly satisfied with having nothing at all. By this process he has no luggage — not even his own body, not even his own mind. He is swallowed up of Jesus Christ. There is nothing of him but Jesus Christ. He has let all his money go, all his opportunities go, all his reputation go — into his money bag, or the honor bag, or the works bag; of others.

This is represented at Jericho by the man who hid his pound because his mind was so set on the marvelous Divine One that he let himself be wiped out. (Verses 20 and 21)

It is not likely that the way this lesson is now about to be interpreted will be acceptable, for the present, to the Sunday-school world; but it is time it was given, for it was the meaning of Jesus. It has revolutionary activity in it without any bloodshed or hiring out of little children to capitalists, that they may get cheap labors and so have more money to build churches and colleges with.

Turn of a Mystic Wheel

This lesson has a wondrous turn of some mystic wheel into the God presence whereby things are wrought out, things are done, things happen, in blessed order, without having to keep some men poor and some men rich by fixing the brains of some with more muscle in them for the knock-down scramble called civilization, which, every bit of it, is the result of pulpit preaching on the usual plan of talking about what Jesus Christ meant.

Just as different from the pulpit interpretation as these Bible lessons are, so different is their influence on the world from the influence of pulpit ministration.

One should be careful to compare last Sunday's lesson with today's. "For when two of you shall agree upon earth as touching any one thing that ye shall ask, it shall be done." So the lessons go by twos. They take the attention above the phenomenal. If we watch the phenomenal we get miserably mixed. If we watch that which is above phenomenon we feel illuminated. The Perean lessons strike out of phenomena altogether, but what they proclaim is indisputable. This lesson swings around its golden text, and is figured out by the man who did no trading with his pound, but, with his thoughts on his Master all full of unworldly praises, he asked only the master, lived only in the master, was lost in the Master.

Notice how he speaks to his Master as one who needs not to plant seed and hoe young stalks for a harvest, because he can take up corn anywhere, find gold anywhere, have whatever he likes any instant.

Notice that he speaks of fearing such a master. Is it not written that the fear of the Lord is the beginning of wisdom? Is it not told that fear of the Lord is simply singleness of eye toward him?

In all texts from any Bible there are allusions to other texts which perhaps are plainer. It is so with this one. Hear the man speak who has no mind only to see his master with concentrated feelings. "I feared thee because thou art an austere man that takest up where thou layest not down, and reapest that thou didst not sow." (Verse 21)

This mighty praise of his Lord causes the pound which he had let lie still to gravitate toward the hardest worker. He is left emburdened with even the face of a penny. He is lost in his Lord. He has been faithful to the least.

How can a man be faithful to the least who is handling much? The whole doctrine of Jesus was humility of the eternal. How humble must we be in order to be least? Truly we must be nothing. So this third one was the man most faithful to the least.

He has permitted himself to be lowly estimated by the world, generation after generation. This, also, is faithfulness to the idea of leastness among men. "He that looketh unto me, though least among men, shall be me."

If there be any one thing taught in the holy Bible it is that of letting the Divine Presence do all things for us and know all things for us. Jesus himself proclaimed: "The words that I speak unto you it is not I that speak, but the Father that dwelleth in me; he doeth the works."

This was surely being faithful to the least. This man, who is the divinest exhibition of being least in simple obedience, let the last vestige of himself be lost that his Lord and the traders might have it all their own way.

Peloubet takes a note from Wells, the scientific translator, where he says that the name of the still element of air, "argon", is the word now used for idle in our language. As for instance: "For every argon word that men shall utter," etc. And what is argon but the move-less, workless third principle in air upon whose eternal steadfastness oxygen and hydrogen feed? What work, what life, what sweetness would oxygen and hydrogen have clashing and coalescing, trading and scrambling, forever, if the argon on its everlasting mission of idleness did not keep its silent promises?

Defense of the Idler in the Parable

Does anybody see any significance in the exposure of the move-less, hitherto unknown argon, and the exposure of the hitherto un-preached doctrine of letting the Divine One be all and all else be nothing, as taught in the sacred books of the ages?

That is by reason of the proclamation of the revealing power in the name Jesus Christ. Names and objects can be affirmed of either audibly or mentally, till finally they are full of the nature of the affirmations. The second man mentioned by

Luke in this chapter represents the practice of charging up objects with great powers, as charms, talismans, etc. In Mexico they have the name Guadalupe charged with prospering and healing energy so manifestly that even foreigners say they see a difference in their environments if they have a genuine Mexican print of Guadalupe in their houses.

The first man mentioned by Luke in this chapter represents the practicing of charging up houses, lands, gold, bank notes, etc. with fictitious values so that the whole march of civilization is swung around the money value of everything. The third man represents the Jesus Christ permission of the divine afflatus to handle the universe from central place to circumference incalculable.

Each set is prospered by reading over this lesson, for each set is working conscientiously on its own plane. Some are working on the Truth plane. They search for truth. They say, that is not truth, this is truth, to sentences and objects. Then whatever they say, they experience. So they are more convinced that they are right than ever. But Jesus at the actual test opened not his mouth and gave up the ghost or the thinking fabric in its truth and error textile. Whoever speaks his name dips his wings into extinction and rises into distinction exactly like Him but without suffering at the lowest point, or ecstasy at the highest point.

Jesus was called wicked and dropped into hell as a common sinner. But he did not stay there. He seemed like Job to be in entire disfavor with the very divine God upon whom his eyes were unflinchingly fixed. So is this third man in this chapter. So are all who let themselves be nothing that the mighty God may be all. To their neighbors God himself seems against them but as Jesus stayed not forever in extinction and corruption it had no lasting affect on his substance, so those who obey like soldiers in the ranks do not mind the erasure of their names in the name they know is the last one to give to the eternal God. If there are multitudes who doubt this interpretation, that will not affect its exactness. In the fullness of the swiftly nearing time when the uncovered Actual spreads itself before mankind, it will be seen as the final one.

There are three planes upon which men operate; viz., physical, mental, divine. They are typified by the three mentioned by Luke in his 19th chapter. The physical passeth away; it is not real. The metaphysical passeth away; it is not real The divine abideth forever the same. The physical multiplieth by exertion, the mental multiplieth by the same. The divine exerteth not itself. He that watcheth the Divine, hath the name of the idler. He getteth much accused. But being faithful to the least, he is fearless.

Inter-Ocean Newspaper, May 17, 1896

LESSON VIII

Unthinkable Divinity

Luke 20:9-19

"Ay free, aff han', your story tell,
When wi' a bosom cronie;
But still keep something to yoursel
Ye scarcely tell to onie" - Burns

*"The stone which the builder rejected is become
the head of the corner." -* Luke, the Physician

The difference between these lessons and other
lessons is that they touch the silent notes in the
Bible sections chosen for international study.
These pick up the seldom-quoted passages of
Scripture, the texts which even the concordance
ignore. One text in point is that one about it being
as great a violence against the Jesus Christ dispensation to kill an ox as a man.

Another is that one about the God eyes, that never behold evil, yet do indeed behold everything there is.

They refer often and often to the ignored doctrine of the unreality of the phenomenal world, the unsubstantial pageantry of nature, with which the Bible is full and which the old philosophers discovered and taught.

They strike over and over on the Bible notes about our having formulated all that we see and touch by using our thinking faculties in the ways we do. They urge, with loving persistence, a change of mind on all things, even to stopping the mind long enough to start it over again with some new premises.

They show, from Sunday to Sunday, how an arm or an eye is bad or good, according to the way the thoughts proclaim it, while it is in a deeper sense something which no thoughts have described. The snake that crawls under your summer tent is a hurtless string, if your mind says so. It is a hurtful thing to most people, because their minds say so. But back of the snake, right in its very skin, shining through its very folds, is a substance which no thoughts ever deal with. It is the unthinkable Divinity, omnipresent.

These lessons deal forever with that unthinkable divinity. They always proclaim its presence. They ring on the golden strings of that heavenly harp that stretches its rhythmic harmonies from zone to zone of the pathless skies and from the heart of man to the drawing heart of the mighty but nameless God.

> "Whereso'er in glory gliding
>   Shine the stars on nights of time,
> There the wondrous magnet hiding.
>   Draweth toward it heart of mine."

These lessons touch the under-currents. Somebody ought to be finding undercurrents and living always with them. Somebody ought to find the key to this universe, and we ought to see by this time that it certainly is not findable along the path of the external and material.

> "The south winds are quick witted,
>   The schools are sad and slow
> The masters quite omitted
>   The lore we care to know."

These lessons, which are called "essay" find that great principle in life of which the schools say nothing; that is, that whatever any woman or man feels to be right and true, even if they do not preach it, will by and by get boldly preached and definitely practiced. Their part in the program is to hold on, endure, never change, never be argued down. Their silent presence will be vital even to the end of the earth. Every sentient creature must feel the influence of their conviction. Such is the mysterious power of abiding unchanging, silent conviction.

All Have Equal Rights

The silent note of the Christian Bible is the equal rights of man to all the gifts of earth and heaven, and that getting more of the things of nature than we need while our neighbors are destitute is highway robbery. The secret principle taught in the Christian Bible is tenderness toward animals. Yet Christian ministers ride after dock-tailed horses, and stew little lambs. And it is nowhere recorded that they preach the equal wages of the boot-black with the school teacher on the ground that each having done the best he could their values are equal on the motive plane.

This is taught as the ethics of Divinity in Scripture. "He shall not judge after the sight of the eyes, nor after the hearing of the ear," as to whether the worked-over object be boots or books, but he shall judge according to the motive. (See Isaiah)

The unstruck chord of Bible lore is that soil our civilization is founded on, the subtle determination in the mind of the hard-brained men to keep as many people in abject poverty as possible, so that they will be glad to do menial services to keep themselves from starvation.

Carnegie says: "To abolish poverty would be to destroy the only soil upon which mankind can depend to produce a higher civilization than we now possess."

But Carnegie is not a moneyless scrub woman, with an underfed brain. How does he know what it might be for the divine civilization if he should keep in his heart the idea that on earth, as in heaven, each could have his equal share, daily apportioned, to do with as he pleased for services rendered, not according to what was done, but according to whether he had done the best his circumstances had allowed? Would life under those conditions be any more worth living to the scrub woman or any less worth living, to Carnegie?

Can anybody imagine what a heavy heel would be lifted off the world if its human hearts could be certain of fair dealings in the matter of returns for faithful efforts? There would be no poverty, to be sure, but how much more wonderful our public buildings, how far more secure our homes, if built and tended by those whose native genius had chosen that kind of labor instead of by those who must do it or starve. This is what the Bible teaches.

Today's lesson repeats last Sunday's idea of the argon, or the power of silent conviction. It tells of how often divine chords are struck by men in the generations, but how quickly even those who felt them most powerfully let go of them, being argued down by appearances. This lesson brings to light, and holds it in the amber of immortal print, the perfectly plain teaching that appearances are so against divine facts that man feels obliged to whip and imprison every divine fact that anybody dare's proclaim

Represents the "Lord" Principle

The "man who planted the vineyard," as here stated, represents the "Lord" principle, that is, the law of cause and effect on every plane of life. The law of cause and effect has not been understood. It has been a long way off from man's mind for a long time. (Verse 9) Particularly on the subject of the Good. The Bible lessons bear to the good, or to that which is above good always.

One good principle which men have whipped every time it has come up is, that as God is omnipresent then that which is not God is nowhere present, and this makes the good so much more powerful than the evil that there is no power whatsoever in evil, So we need not fight evil at all. Jesus of Nazareth taught this by saying, "Let the dead bury their dead follow thou me." "I am life, love, spirit, kindness." "I will give you rest."

This was no new principle, but how did the people of the world use it? We all know that they do to this day watch death, sickness, pestilence, microbes, material dangers, and poverty. They fight them by close attention to them, and trying to overcome them on their own plane. They reject the offer of a presence all life, love, kindness, able to dissolve death, disease, danger. They to this day punish that offer whenever anybody makes it. (Verse 10) They insist on overcoming nature's apparent obstacles by their own methods. Ages of misery as the result of whipping that message do not seem to teach the world to charge it off.

The second servant, or principle, offered to man every generation is that man is the creator of the world in which he lives, and may have his surroundings fortunate or terrible, according to the way he handled his mind. That by a change of mind his old world will whiff away and become a new world.

"Then shall thy world grow polar to thee, slowly taught,
And crystal out a new world like thy thought."

Strange as it may seem, men have always whipped and slashed this message. And, strange as it may seem, no man has ever held his ground on it as a working fact who has ever discovered it. Schopenhauer found that his world was his own make up, caused by his mind, but he never offered to change his mind, and thereby rejuvenate and repopulate his world. He forgot his propositions on this principle as fast as he made them. From Pythagoras down, the philosophers who found out this law of life could not keep their personal ground upon it. Read them over and see. You will find the punished message under their discussion of the reality and substantiality of the material world.

The third wonderful principle offered by certain inspired hearts as a straight message from the Lord fact in life is that man, by stopping his thoughts and senses and turning to face his own starting point, behind him, would find his backward vision lighted up by a new fire; would cut off his sight of this whole universe and see into the heaven, where he hailed from originally. "Look unto me and be ye saved." "The kingdom of God is within you." "The I AM hath sent thee." "Turn unto me."

This is the most absurd principle probably ever offered to man. Its very absurdity has been its majesty, for its simplicity is its evidence of the direct gaze of the Almighty toward man. As yet it has had no representative, one holding it against all opposition and showing plainly that he was secured, himself, to its safety from the hurts of the world. (Verse 12)

Reached Its Splendor In Jesus Christ

Last of ail, it is true that, as all the great reasonings of the ages reached their capstone in Socrates, and all the beauty concepts of time bloomed in Phidian marbles, so all the understanding of the Divine Presence ever felt by man reached its splendor in Jesus of Nazareth. He understood God so well that He was God. "For none of thy good works do we atone thee, but because thou, being a man, makest thyself God." He understood man so well that He was man. Thus He was man understanding God, and God understanding man. He took upon himself all the infirmities of man and dissolved them in his God substance. He took into his own body all the sickness of man and all the foolishness of man, all the poverty of man, all the blindness, all the iniquity, all the pain, all the death, and, in the mighty alchemy of his God body, He transfigured flesh and bone and sinew, both of mind and matter, into a substance undefiled, that fadeth not away. He made the startling offer to all the earth that no man need struggle any more with sin, sickness, or death. His struggle and his victory had achieved all things for all men. There never need be any ignorance or pain, any study to learn God, or any religion to follow out, for his finding of God and his presence everywhere forever, should be enough for all mankind. (Verse 13)

So here are four great messages straight from the Lord strength that has its seat somewhere. Not one of them has been received by anybody ever showing on this earth as a human being. This last one, the offer of a man who had practiced the first three principles in rapid succession with great results, has been the worst treated, the least understood, of any of the messages. (Verse 15)

Now, the grip of the evil on man, being caused by his believing in it, has reached such a stage that this lesson hints there is now no dissolving it by accepting the first three messages and carrying them out ever so faithfully. There is now no freedom, except by the Son. "But if the Son shall make you free, you shall be free indeed."

This lesson puts the facts of human existence into plain terms; shows how real and hard human existence seems to be, and shows how to set it aside as nothing at all by four easy methods, the last one being easiest of all. It shows how we must all keep up the force of seeming to suffer and die on the material plane until we strike onto some one of these great offers and stand to it. It shows that the final offer does not come until after the other three have had their rejected preachers on the earth. This section of Luke acts as a hard blow on man to call his attention to the security from earthly bondages of all sorts, which is his by divine right.

It puts a straight experience through which we shall go with all the vividness of reality if we do not take notice of the four messages always being proclaimed in some unpretentious fashion on our earth and herein recorded.

(Verse 16) The final offer is the capstone or final principle on the plane of dealing with cause and effect. There is no disputing that there is cause and its consequence whilesoever human existence makes itself manifest. And on this plane there are these four simple plans of escape from them, the teeth of mental errors.

Was Offered as a Substitute
The life of Jesus of Nazareth was deliberately offered as a substitute for other men's lives. Whether it was a sensible, majestic noble thing to do, and whether it was a successful undertaking can only be proved by some one who accepts it, as it reads. If I die, then I have not accepted his offer, for according to the way the Bible reads, he died once, and that exempts me from going through that operation.

If I am foolish, or ignorant, or in trouble, or if I am a failure in any respect, than I have not accepted his offer, for according to the way the Bible reads he bore all these miseries once, and that exempts me from bearing them. I go free. So, If I am struggling to find my divine self, or practicing any formulae or breathings or axioms in the hope of being more concentrated to my "I Am", the divine presence, I have not accepted his offer, for according to the way the Bible reads He went through all those tasks once and found the Absolute, and in his finding I am exempt from duty to practice anything to find God. I go free.

This is the last of the cause and effect Lord. Upon accepting this, the father and I are one in body and mind. Nobody need say that such teaching is not plainly in the Christian Bible, for it is. If there is anything to criticize about it, go back and settle it with Luke or Mark or John. I am not to blame for it. Any more than I am to blame for the prima &.ce evidence we have all about us that the first three messages were well taught, by what were called Christian Scientists, and poverty, pain, and quarreling have held high Carnival, just the same. The old-fashioned church tells us that if Jesus suffered, it is our duty to suffer, if he died, then we must die. If he was spit upon and hurt, then we must be spit upon also.

But the Bible does not teach this way. It teaches vicarious atonement or the setting free of all men by the freedom of one man, the welding of

all men into the God substance by the manifestation of God in the body of one man: and the
resurrection of all men from out their dying and
dark minded ways into eternal life and unburdened peace here and now without doing anything
to earn it. The Bible teaches me that I do not have
to earn my freedom. It is already earned. That I do
not have to get at one with the mind that is God by
any process. The at-one-ment, or at one mind, has
been made.

It is not a question of what one believes. It is
an honest rendering of what the Bible teaches,
which one must make when reading it. One cannot
call himself a Christian who believes in suffering
in any form. He belongs to verse 16 of this chapter.
He has not accepted either of the three servants or
the son.

The son offer is the one we must accept all by
ourselves alone with the unbearable sorrows of our
lot which no science of mind has ever utterly ame-
liorated for anybody. There is surely some plan of
exemption, setting free, balm, or surcease. The
Bible makes the offer of the Jesus Christ plan. If it
is not a good one it has the merit at least, that it is
more comradeship, compassion, benevolence, tol-
eration, warmth in it, than the three philosophical
propositions of Christian Science, called "servants"
in the 20th chapter of Luke.

Inter-Ocean Newspaper, May 24, 1896

LESSON IX

The Destruction Of Jerusalem Foretold

Luke: 21:20-36

The subject for today's study is "The Destruction of Jerusalem Foretold". Whenever Jerusalem is mentioned it symbolizes the "I Am" of each of us. Sometimes the real and changeless "I Am", sometimes the fleeting end unsubstantial "me". We are to hear the story of the fleeting and unsubstantial today; how it may be transfigured into the glorious and eternal by one process, how it may pass through gloom and annihilation by another. By one process there is suffering; by the other there is freedom from pain.

Last Sunday's lesson told of three philosophical propositions that have appeared among men with a scheme for helping the world out of suffering, all of which have been rejected in every age, and always will be rejected. Also it told of a fourth firm and astonishing proposition, very tangible and unphilosophical, which also is rejected now, has been rejected in the past, and always will be rejected. It is true that a few people of this world have undertaken to accept them, but their examples have not been encouraging enough to wile on the millions upon millions upon the globe.

Now, Jesus of Nazareth tells what happens to each of us on our external human, mortal flesh, intellect, carnal plane, when it is not attending strictly to the divine plane and letting the divine plane manage its destiny without opposition. Jerusalem of Judea, in the time of Jesus, acted exactly like the ordinary mind everywhere, through all time and wound up exactly as the ordinary mind must wind up when it is not giving the Divine Presence complete sway.

The lesson gives some few people the credit of attending to the Divine Presence closely enough so that nothing happened to them at all like what happened to the rest of the people. It tells that it is true that nobody is ever lost, or dies, to his own consciousness, but his experiences are exactly as if he did, if he does not go the straight path of his divine "I Am". There is no use of going around by the hands and curves of trouble, pain, death, etc., but all can travel home by those circuitous tracks who want to. This lesson declares that the stuff called personal will, with which we are all more or less thickened, will march us in straight contrariness to our own advantages.

It is a very subtle lesson in its manner of pointing out the way to stand up in the majesty of our native greatness, for it makes a whole city represent our personal self-will at its daily task of cropping out on every occasion, in everything we do, and in all our human relations. It makes a few silent men and women represent the presence of the divine will, able to do all things, but never taking the lead and overpowering everything till the personal will lets go.

Here is Jerusalem, representing personal will, never letting go, and Jesus, having his eyes on the heavenly Jerusalem, or the divine will, which never projects itself, and, therefore, never gets into any fights.

The Jerusalem of this story typifies the intellectual world, with its material tastes. This is the personal will at its common business. There is no record of anybody ever having given up his personal will to the divine will (except in rare moments) but Jesus of Nazareth. He declared, from first to last, that he had utterly let go of his personal will. "I came not to do mine own will; my will is His that sent me."

If we bring up old martyrs as evidences of giving up personal will, we shall see that they were the stiffest-necked fighters against God that we could possibly name. Every one of them spoke ill of everybody and everything. Every one of them declared himself in the right and everybody else in the wrong as long as he could gasp. In rare mo-

ments he would say that the divine God made all
things, but to him they were mostly owned by the
other party, whose name was the opposite of God.
Having smelted his will to opposing the freedom of
his neighbors, he, of course, opposed his own freedom.

Absolute, unconditioned freedom is the divine
will. Whoever opposes freedom opposes the divine
will by setting up his material Jerusalem. Read
over the 21st chapter of Luke, which is today's
lesson, particularly from Verses 20 to Verse 36,
and there you have the signs of the dissolution of
the fluctuating human will after it has declined to
give itself up peaceably.

There is one mighty presence everywhere. Its
messages have been spoken plainly by men in
certain moments of inspiration, when the lightnings of the silent divine have run through the
glooms of earthly sounds and struck them. "The
eternal God is thy refuge," "Acknowledge me, and I
will direct thy paths." That eternal presence is the
New Jerusalem. But this lesson proclaims that
that personal, intellectual will of the world will
never acknowledge meekly the supreme ability of
the divine power. Therefore, it must experience
violence. It chooses violence when it stands up for
itself. Old Jerusalem was the type of each of us
and our history.

Verse 20 declares that armies of disagreeable
and threatening infirmities finally lay hold of the
self-willed personality! And whenever they have

become so positive that they make every little thing and every great thing a hateful movement, we can be certain of some climax.

This is true of every personality. He is coming rapidly to something momentous when first one thing and then another happens to discourage and hurt him. It is in this lesson declared to be true of the final winding-up of the whole farce of personal will on this earth. Each man, each woman shall have so much trouble, so much discouragement, that he or she shall not know which way to turn.

Is there any way for people to elude these troubles? Yes, Verse 21 says: "Let them flee to the mountains." Where is that? The highest proclamations that we have ever heard or known or felt. Out of all the wonderful things told about the divine will there must have been one or two or three that have attracted the attention. These, having attractive power, can pull the whole man out of the difficulty. They are as magnetic as mountain tops to climbers. Many a business man has written himself through disasters and come safely out, business and himself intact. They wrote on paper the best things they knew. They kept their minds on those best things and those best things lifted them out and up on fine, invisible ropes.

"Flee as a bird to the mountains."
"Let them which are in the midst of it (the city) depart out."

It seems as if we must struggle and fight with destinies, with afflictions: encounter them face to face. Not at all. Let them alone. "Depart out." During the siege of Jerusalem of Judea, A.D. 66, which was set to prefigure the overthrow of personal will, those who had their eyes fixed on the Divine Presence had divine warning to leave the city. They took advantage of the time when Cestius Gallus so mysteriously withdrew his array from the walls at a moment when by a single stroke he might have taken the city.

There has never been any explanation of why the commander so hastily withdrew and did not take advantage of his opportunity. No evil, no violence, can take place in the vicinity of a man whose eye is on his God. Cestius Gallus was drawn away by those invisible cords which were pulling the lover of Jesus Christ out of Jerusalem. They fled between the two sieges, A.D. 66 and 69.

Lo! in the day of the demolition of personal ambition, fix thine eye on high. The crash and rumble of falling people shall not then be known to thee. Bands of fine light shall pull on thee and wing thy feet. Cords of sweet influence shall draw on thee and lift thy weightless body into safety.

Verse 22 declares that all demolition is vengeance. So is the burning of a hand put into the fire. It is the law of cause and effect. The effect is always vengeance, whether it is pleasant or hateful. This lesson reiterates that there is something ahead of vengeance; some thing that can annul effects of causes. People talk about selfishness causing some bodily tightness. This is talking about vengeance. Jesus was forever lifting the attention to that Mighty One who can undo vengeance in a twinkling.

"So then," you exclaim, "you are so foolish as to say that there is some principle which can stop fire from burning." Yea. "When thou passeth through the rivers they shall not overflow, when thou passeth through the fires they shall not burn thee, neither shall the flames kindle upon thee." "The eternal God is thy refuge." This is not what happens to anybody studying material things. He always catches their fires and floods, their cancers and earthquakes.

Lionel Beale told Joseph Cook that there ought to be something to upset natural law. The Christian Bible tells what will upset natural law. Its last message on that point was mentioned at the closing of last Sunday's lesson. Today's lesson alludes to it, but talks to people on the verge of calamity for not having accepted any of the offers of escape, and also to those who have gladly taken up with the last offer. Those who have taken up with the last offer do not catch any calamity as a contagion from other men's calamities. They go free.

Verse 23 tells of the woes of the mothers in the days of vengeance; gives the way of free flight for the mothers in the days of escape from natural law. Motherhood has the hardest time of anything on this planet, especially human motherhood. Nature, man, and civilization combine to hurt her.

This is the effect of a cause. Or in the words of Verse 22, it is vengeance.

Why is this? It is because mothers believe everything they are told. As they are told principles whose effects are crushing, they must wind up under the car of juggernaut, according to the law of being bodily affected by mental beliefs; a run of things to which all the earth is subjected if out of direct touch with Divine Presence.

On the symbolic, or illustrative physical plane, how hard for mothers to run and climb mountains. On the mental plane, how hard for a mind to stop giving heed (or suck, Verse 23) to doctors' stories about the diseases to which people are liable; how hard to stop giving nourishing attention to philanthropists' stories about the degradation and wickedness of the world; how hard to atop giving attention (which is all the nourishment they need) to the school-men's theories about the ignorance of the world how hard to flee mentally to lofty mountains of free Bible texts, when loaded down in mind with much information about matter, misery, ignorance, etc.

On the mental plane, anybody is a mother who believes and gives attention to anything told to the people on this earth about the power of evil against good. On the mental plane a man is just as much a woman in this respect as anybody. For on the mental plane men give credence to lies. There is a fine set of lies about sex differences, caste differences, natural differences of all sorts, which the world is loaded down with.

This lesson declares, in substance, that there is neither male nor female in Christ Jesus. They are all equally free to run to the mountain tops of divine safety. There is neither black nor white in Christ Jesus. They are all equally free to flee from the shades of ignorance. "The Holy Ghost whom the Father will send in my name, shall teach them all equally well."

In Verse 24 it tells again of the physical plane as always showing out how the mental plane is thinking. For old Jerusalem should have swords and prisons to expose how cutting and binding the people's thoughts had been. That verse explains how cruel and clutching ideas do come back upon those who started them up. It is just as if men were their own vengeance makers.

The Jews hated the gentiles and the gentiles hated the Jews. Now comes the vengeance or consequence. But the great Free One stands there. Unto Him the audience are looking. And in his freedom they go free. They had been Jewish haters, but now they hate no more and this former hatred is erased. They go free from material swords and mental prisons; with a freedom not like the freedom of our colored slaves bought by fighting and paralyzing a nation, not like the freedom of America seized by mowing down the British. It was the mysterious freedom of the Jesus Christ fightless, unassailable safety.

In Verse 25 it tells how the sun, moon, and stars all tremble when man is perturbed; how they faint and fall when man is secretly afraid. For, although the eternal sun shall never tremble on its stately march, the sun with which men by their minds do hide the Eternal One, can grow dark and hide, or can glow and smile to keep tally with the changeable moods of man. And though the ever-lasting stars can never flicker resting on their changeless beds of solemn black, those stars; with which man's minds do hide the never-endingness, do often flare up and fall to signify how man, as one mind on a globe, has dropped some hope. And, though the fadeless, steadfast earth can never reel, that earth described by the minds of man "shall reel to and fro like a drunken man," said the prophet to point how unstable is the confidence of man on a globe as one mind, in the sure care of the father, the divine will.

In the confidence of Jesus Christ, those who heard him caught the contagion of confidence. And in the reeling days of besieged Jerusalem they were free from danger.

The last verses, without doubt, refer as much to this age as to Anno Domini 69. For now is come the close of personal will on this earth. Some shall lose it by violence, some by surrender.

The Czar may cover himself with insignia of office to awe the world into admiration of his personal will. Victoria may command her subjects to pay and pay and pay tithes to her caparisoned family. Cleveland may despise the poor of his country; the corporations may squeeze their mill-wheels to silence, to awe the laboring multitudes but one and all must give up their personal aims, determinations, wills. The closing of the old dispensation began when the entirely new preaching of Jesus Christ started. And it is now being noted for its banners and signals resembling closely those which hung out in the days of dissolving the Jerusalem of Judea 1800 years ago.

Thus does history repeat itself, each time on a larger scale? This time the whole world is Jerusalem of Judea. Thus a whole world winds up some prevailing characteristic representing the personal determinations of each human being to have his own way about every single thing he deals with. And where are the preachers, the teachers, with fire enough from the altar of safety in them to show that the loss of the personal will into the competent divine will does not mean loss of intelligence or power, neither does it mean pain and trouble, but it means new wisdom, supernal power, winged freedom from struggle and sorrow.

Verse 27 tells of seeing the divine God face to face, and so, of course not being able to see anything else. This verse hints that though at the symbolic siege of the City of Solomon only a handful escaped from the sword, yet, at the final destruction of materiality with its personal wills which made it, all the people of the earth shall be forgiven for not having ever accepted any of the schemes for escaping misery, and, through sight of the free Jesus Christ, shall all go free.

Verse 28 reads as though forgiveness shall forever mean 'giving for'. It reads as though all men should gladly let go of their present clutchings, both mental and physical, and let the Mighty One have it all his own way. His will be given in place of their clutching determinations.

Then Jesus added a parable concerning the full fig tree — meaning the end of the effects started by a set of causes. The end of delusion. The fullness of time, for all things that appear. In Verse 36 he gives the one direction with which all the lessons have gleamed for more than a year "Watch". For whatsoever we watch we do certainly see it move. We see its laws. Agassiz watched the rocks and beasts of earth, and they gave him many of their secrets. Solomon said that little ants have wise teachings for men. He advised watching ants. Surgeons in hospitals advise watching bones. Doctors advise watching diseases. A New York society watches wasps. Another watches thoughts of the personal mind to see how they eventuate. But Jesus taught watching God.

The great way of escape from the mass of conditions, both mental and physical, which we are now clutching so vigorously, is repeated in this Verse 36. It is a treatment to call attention to the way of absolute freedom. We loose our life from the snares of our own personal determinations by watching the changeless, untrammeled spirit that

bloweth where it listeth and can never be held in
bondage by us, though our own wills should be as
tenacious and muscular as Nero's or Napoleon's.
These lessons practically declare that nobody ever
voluntarily gives up his will to the divine will,
because he has the conditions of mind and body
glued to him so tightly that he has no mind to do it
with; but they tell plainly that watching the
Mighty Presence at our right hand, at our left
hand, under our feet, never leaving us, will loose
our bonds, will set us free. Though we know not
the name of this everlasting Presence, yet attending to it will give us free escape.

Some people object to calling the nameless
presence "It". They would tie us to the word "Him".
Some object to calling this nameless presence
"Him". They would tie us to "Her".

But this Presence is not hurt by our miscalling,
nor helped by our stiff-necked dogmatics. Jesus,
the wonderful knower of God, gave him no gender,
neither masculine nor feminine, nor neuter.
"Watch" — that was all. "Watch" till unhindered
ye, like Jesus, can lay down your body and take it
up again. Watch, till untrammeled ye, like Jesus,
can rise on the wings of the morning. Watch, till
unclutching the fingers of both mind and body ye,
like him, have left earth's binding shells of pain on
the banks of "time's un-resting sea".

Watch, till vision hath been lighted with fire
from on high. Watch, till yet flee on free wings to
the mountains. Watch, till ye rest undisturbed on

the silent lightnings of spirit. Watch, till there is sunshine in your arteries, and not iron. Watch, till the day dawn and the shadows flee away.

"Unto you, O men, I call, and my voice is to the sons of man."

Inter-Ocean Newspaper May 31, 1896

LESSON X

"Forgiveness For Hunger"

Luke: 22:24-37

The proper subject of this lesson is "Forgiveness for Hunger." The Committee of Decision do not so call it. They say it is a solemn warning. This discourse, which surveys the kindly promise of forgiveness for hunger, was delivered by Jesus of Nazareth Thursday evening, April 6, about twenty hours before his crucifixion. (The calendar arranged by the religious world reads this way respecting the last three days of the career of Jesus:

1. The days of privacy, Wednesday and Thursday, April 5 and 6, at Bethany.
2. The Lord's supper, Thursday evening, April 6.
3. The last discourse (John) Thursday evening, April 6.
4. The prayer, Thursday evening, April 6.
5. Gethsemane, midnight, April 6.
6. The betrayal early Friday morning, probably 1 o' clock, April 7.

The carefully taught disciples had been quarreling as to who was greatest among them. (Luke 22:24-37) They had the world-hunger for adulation. One is not cured of any hunger until the vacuum is filled. This filling of a vacuum is religiously termed "forgiveness."

The ceremony of feet washing had no adulation in it for the disciples of Jesus till he injected honor into it. Thereafter, even to this day, there is considerable pomp attended with it. Instance, holy week, in Rome, when the Pope has his hunger for adulation fed with a moiety (one of two equal parts) thereof, as in the presence of people of the proudest rank he washes the feet of a few aged paupers. For his hunger he has to "feed". It is ministered unto him by the adulation of rank. It is the forgiveness principle as interpreted by the Satanic Prince of this world through his best disciples.

This lesson, like last Sunday's, exhibits the "two" plane: right and left; black and white, male and female, mind and matter, high and low. It shows up the Satanic Prince of this world forgiving hunger, and the good Lord of this world forgiving hunger. It strikes hard on the promise, "They shall hunger no more; neither thirst any more," but unless the ears have been cured of double deafness they cannot hear the sound of this blow.

That state where people never hunger or thirst, is a third state, belonging to the purely Jesus Christ dispensation. It takes us beyond the time of the filling of empty spaces, even with righteousness. There was a set of people to whom Jesus said, "Blessed are they that do hunger and thirst after righteousness for they shall be filled." This lesson tells secretly and adroitly about what happens to those "filled" people at the state where they know no hunger for anything, any more at all.

It is not an imaginable state. There is no Vanderbilt, or Gould, or Armour, or Pullman but what is hungering and thirsting after something the whole time. Some of them even exchange their children for foreign titles in the vain hope that this hunger may be fed. Some try other most extraordinary ways of filling their mental esophagus — all to no lasting purpose. Today's lesson describes the hunger of the twelve picked disciples of Jesus, and how Judas swallowed the honorable place at the table, supposed to have feeding grain in it for the alimentary canal known as ambition.

But Judas soon found that his empty space was still empty, for Jesus himself stepped down and washed the feet of the twelve men companioning him. As he was then acknowledged to be the greatest and wisest in every way, His taking the dishonored place of menial made the end seat at table no great bread to feed ambition with.

His Hunger had Been Fed

By this action Jesus of Nazareth taught that his ambition hunger had been utterly fed. By associating with thieves and harlots he exhibited the fact that his social hunger had been appeased. By declining to be known as a leader of the Greek schools of philosophy he showed that he was not hungry to be known as equal to Socrates or Plato. What had he been fed with that he was sufficient unto himself in all these particulars? His own reply was, "I have meat to eat that ye know not of." And it is more than evident that nobody knows that meat to this very day, for such a hungry set as the creatures on this globe are can scarcely be duplicated on any of the other globes. Do not try to show up any of the so-called Christian people as fed while they still long for the conversion of the world to their way of thinking. Do not show up the Buddhists as fed while they are gasping after Nirvana. Those all need forgiveness for hunger.

The state of actual forgiveness, where one is self-sufficient, having life in himself to keep himself alive forevermore, having health in himself to keep himself wholesome forever, having wisdom in himself to inform himself without end of knowledge, is what Jesus Christ had. Is there any doubt about that? He called this limitless well within himself "the Father." At this Father center he was not hungry to have the world happy, for the instant he touched it he retired from the sight of the world and let them hunger after him to this day

This chapter of Luke was meant to tell us that mystery of self- sufficingness. If we do not catch the mystery there is no God to care for our vacuum. For even the actual Being that fills heaven and earth is not desirous of our knowing him enough so that he tells us his name. Shelley wrote as long ago as 1811, "The word of God, a vague word, has been, and will continue to be, the source of numberless errors, till it is erased from the nomenclature of philosophy." Jesus Christ offered his own name as competent to feed the world. "I am that bread." but he did not urge it. He said he was sufficient forgiveness for a world. But he did not go about preaching or healing one single minute after he touched the self-supplying fountain within his own self. He lets us scramble around and seek him and his meanings. He is not hungering after our recognition any more at all forever.

Verse 25 declares that benefactors are only hungry men in disguise. They desire and want and gnaw and maw and chew after governship, authority. Whoever does us a favor makes us quail as much as he can. This feeds some vacant spots in him: "And he said unto them, the Kings of the gentiles exercise lordship over them; and they that exercise authority upon them are called benefactors." Probably Queen Victoria thinks she is a benefactor. The Czar is also laboring under that delusion. The younger rulers of nations are quite a little fed by the praises they get; as benefactors. Jesus Christ was not deceived by the people's deception on this point, nor by the governor's assumptions. He knew that benefaction was the world's satanic lords of good and evil scumming over the self-ability within each man of the masses. He knew that, being himself undeceived, his presence forever on this earth would be eye-opening for all who should know him through time.

"He will destroy the face of the covering cast over all people, and the veil that is spread over all nations."

Above all things, do not try to be a benefactor to the race. For the day cometh when the race will know it as a scheme on your part to lord it over them.

The cessation of this effort starts up the secret inward feeding foundations.

Verse 26 shows that the less we try to be great, important, rich, pompous, the greater we shall be. And the greater we are the more efficient we are. For the hunger for size of some sort, we have actual size. Hot size pasted on us by being praised, but the springing up of limitless might from the deeps of our being where the unnamed wonder forever abides. There is no age to this ever-springing glory. It is impossibly young. "He that is greatest among you let him be as the younger."

Is Hunger for Authority

Next to ceasing from trying to feed the hunger for doing good, which, let us not forget, is only a bogus name for hunger for authority, is ceasing from the hunger to be known as a great character, or mighty power. This is disguised by the apparently benevolent wish to provide employment for the masses. Hundreds of industrial schools are marked examples of manual training promoters. Whenever we hear people talking about providing employment for the masses it is their sly manner of hiding their hunger to be called great. It is their decoy. If they are successful they hire many thousands of fellow-beings to trudge along with dinner pails. Cease from wanting to employ anybody. This cessation starts up an inward fountain with limitless greatness in its nourishing waters. Do not try to be great by wise manipulations of human beings. Be great from the rise of the unending force of the native soul, spirit, heart. One day all men shall know employers of men to be only lovers of increase by authority, hungerers after superiority, thirsters after greatness. For those they are employing shall know how to rise from their own fountains and provide for themselves. "He that is chief, as he that doth serve." The present chief and the present servant, one and the same in self-guiding ability, and neither dependent on the other.

Verse 27 explains that there was no man at table whom Jesus did not declare to be equal to himself. Yet he was performing the arduous task of bathing their feet. He could sit and receive or he could do the work. It did not exalt or demean him. He was unassailable greatness. We are all privileged to be that. It is in us to be what we were in the beginning, and with the exhibition of that there is no hunger to be thought great. "I am among you as he that serveth." The menial and I are one. I am as I am and he is as he is. Each doth know his own fountain — or father.

Verse 28 talks of temptations. This can be interpreted physically, metaphysically, or divinely. Physically, temptations touch the appetites and other actions. Metaphysically temptations are thoughts that pull the mind away from a focus. The Orientals practice breathings to keep the mind concentrated. Divinely, temptations are attentions toward the ever-springing fountain of original sweetness that lies at our center of being, at our right hand, at our left hand, under our feet. Its presence is its own attraction; there is no outer show of the twelve faculties of Jesus bending toward his central springs. Once having started the attention that way there was no stopping it. "Let us not into temptation." (Which we are told was the way the Lord's prayer first read), means truly that the wonderful One never lets us get away. Thou lettest us not away.

This man Jesus had kept his twelve powers plainly in use while yet he was attending his own divine center. He never was in a trance. Nobody ever controlled him, whether astral form or bodily man. When it speaks of his being led of the spirit it means that his own mind made a choice. Each of the twelve disciples stood for one particular conscious power felt by Jesus.

Verse 29 says that each power has its own mission, which it does not fulfill well till all the twelve powers of man together have dipped their oars back into the original "I Am" at the headquarters of each man. Therefore it is not until twelve men, each representing conscious inspiration through some one of the twelve forces of man, have simultaneously faced their original divinity that the actual God is manifest. The story of Jesus and his twelve men, the story of Krishna and his twelve men, the story of Jacob and his twelve sons, the story of Charlemagne and his twelve paladins, are all meant to tell about these twelve powers. Every man has twelve acquaintances who represent always to him just how much practical efficiency his mind has touched.

Will be Able to Foresee

Verse 30 tells that there shall be some man in full conscious inspiration and with him shall be twelve mighty efficient influences. This man shall extend his vision so far that he can foresee; shall extend his hearing so far that he shall forehear, shall extend his mind so far that he shall foreknow, and all the silly theories of the present age shall tremble. There are signals of such a being already started out.

Some of the seemingly most impregnable sciences of the schools are getting their heads off by the knowledges that are flying from different directions. There have been one hundred sudden proofs lately that the world is not a globe and does not revolve. There have been some bold convictions that the writers of the Bible with their extended sights were more accurate than Kepler or Copernicus.

"He hath set the world upon pillars" (1 Samuel) "God, who founded the earth on its basis that it should not be moved forever and aye" (which is the Hebrew text for Psalms XCIII, 1). These hundred proofs etc. are now being circulated from Longon (J. Williams, No. 32 Bankside S.E. 10 cents). But the text book on astronomy is not the only school book about to pass into limbo. All the tribes are to be judged.

Verse 31 tells of the Peter time of the world hidden by mistakes and errors till it gets some light straight from headquarters. Satan is the reign of the present systems of government, religion, finance. They are the direct opposites of the Jesus Christ dispensation. They are the scramble of the world to feed itself by every process devisable except by the exhibition of the divine power resident in all men equally.

Verse 32 says, "When thou art converted strengthen the brethren." It is the intellect that must convert or turn around first. None of the other powers can be strong if the intellect is against them. Intellect is that faculty which takes a premise and jumps at a conclusion. It premises that the earth rotates and then accounts for the rise of the sun in the east from that premise. It states that man is a crawling worm, and then declares he must perish by decay. If he states that man is divine he will see divinity everywhere. If he says he never knew Jesus Christ he will go out and weep bitterly because of separation from his Lord.

Verse 33 shows how the positive assertion of any proposition can only be carried out into uninterested proof when two are steadily agreed. Peter said his say. Jesus denied it. But he denied it only for one day. He resumed his concurrence later on. This represents family life. The husband says his say. The wife opposes. This makes a hitch and tangle in their affairs somewhere. Later on the wife concurs. Then affairs begin to straighten. Let one or the other have his or her say and let the other stand to it. This will be prosperity. There is tremendous success in harmony of statement. "When two of you shall agree upon earth as touching any one thing it shall be done." Jesus always dealt with Peter on the substance of the word. Verse 34 says, whatever he states he sees it formulated. He is the power of the word. The Roman Catholic Church is founded on the power of the word. Whatever they have proclaimed, that they have had come to pass, good or bad. Each of us has this power of the word to use in praise of the present Satanic systems or the present Jesus Christ exhibition.

Verses 35 and 36 tell of the days when the devil side of the world seems to have all the success; then the more cruel a man is, the more he has his own way; the more cheating a man does, the more money he has, the more shrewd he is at cornering the productions of the earth, the greater his reputation. But that state of affairs on earth is only pro tempore. During its reign however, the saint side of mankind will have to handle money and school books and explanations exactly, to all appearances, like the rest of the world, while yet knowing that all that comes to them is divinely tendered. These Bible lessons have proclaimed, latterly, that these gentle and generous-hearted ones are now about to be the only successful ones on the planet.

Verse 37 shows how those who have been termed transgressors because they have seemed not to succeed against the Satanic pressures have one final climax, and then they know the whole process of hardship has been nothing at all. The things concerning evil stop, have an end. The .world that hurts, whether mentally or bodily, stops; it swings its shadows to right and left.

"And on the morn that then springs clear
　　No night can ever fall."

The end of hiding the divine power and glory at the headquarters of man comes. On the brink of time its efforts to feed with husks are ceased. At the edge of the earth its bread and meat are behind us. We must eat of the same meat that Jesus had or starve. There is an old prophecy that reads about things being on the edge of eternity when the earth teems with plenty and the productions are all cheap enough, but the multitudes can have none. They must then be forgiven for hunger.

Inter-Ocean Newspaper, June 7, 1896

LESSON XI

"Forgiveness For The Unknown And The Undone"

Luke: 23:33-46

The subject of this day's lesson is "Forgiveness for the unknown and the undone."

David asks, "Who can understand his errors?" The answer to this question is: nobody. Then there is no use searching around after causes of evil, for they cannot be found. The springs of divine beauty, health, strength, peace are findable. Whoever finds them has forgiveness for what he does not know. The machinery that can move mountains without the touch of a finger or employment of a drudge is reachable. Whoever reaches it has forgiveness for what he has not done.

Lavater narrates an experience where, "being in great distress over some school exercises full of errors which he could not correct, he addressed the airs around him, all charged with wisdom. When his papers reached the schoolmaster they had been unaccountably corrected. He had been for-given for the undone. A new intelligence filled him concerning the propositions involved. This was forgiveness for the unknown.

On the cross Jesus did not ask the universal wisdom to teach the multitudes their mistakes. He asked it to charge them with forgetfulness of what they had seemed to do, and to charge them with glorified knowledge where they had seemed to expose ignorance." (Luke 23:33-46)

As his requests were always answered we may know that those people will never be held account-able for nailing him to the cross while carrying out their ignorance. They said: "His blood be on us and our children." But they did not directly address the divine Intelligence and Operator of the universe when they said that, so there was no charge of everlasting substance in their words. Their very meaning was lost and in its place is the living spray of understanding of omnipotence that every descendant of theirs does now possess.

This experience of Jesus of Nazareth was the eleventh in his series of twelve practical illustra-tions. At this point he voluntarily took upon himself the worst punishment for crime ever prac-ticed on mankind. They did not know why he, who was so powerful, did not interpose to save himself. They did nothing to liberate him. And, through all time, nobody should ever know why he took that way to illustrate his purpose. And nobody should ever do anything to mitigate the sufferings of the left balance of humanity.

The only knowledge possible to man is knowledge of God, which comes as a free gift. The only works man can do are done for him by the free movement of Almighty God. Mankind were believing in themselves as trespassers when Jesus got among them. They believed strongly in terrible punishments for their trespasses. They did not know why they were sinners, nor how to elude punishments. They believed strongly in temporary absolution of wickedness by the scapegoat process. The book of Leviticus tells their formulas for temporary atonement, temporary forgiveness. A live goat was sent into the wilderness with the burden of all sins laid upon him. (Lev. 16:21)

Jesus undertook to be the scapegoat of the world, not for temporary absolution of trespasses, but for eternal freedom therefrom. It was so stupendous an undertaking that it shook the heavens with awe. It was so mighty an offer to man that the rocks rent with astonishment.

Jesus undertook to uprise from the grave by the uplifting energy of the unkillable to God in himself, to show other men through all time how deathless they all are. He claimed that by his thus voluntarily and consciously rising by the energy of divinity, he should have power enough to make all other men fully aware forever of the rising spirit they had within themselves, so that they need never descend into the grave as he had done, but might throw off the garments of old age, sickness, violence, and renew their strength, beauty, wisdom, right here, now.

<u>Lessons That Should Be Learned</u>

In his risen strength they should be risen strength. In his risen glory they should be always glorious. The proposition was so great that the whole earth reeled under it. The claim was so far reaching that the sun bowed himself down for it to pass over him on its stopless journey.

If anybody will make any claim concerning himself, and back himself up by continual insistence that the omnipotent God is his authority, he will do wonders on this earth. He must stand to his claim. He must not be bluffed or backed down by opposition, sneers, accusations, seeming failures, or losses. This will cause him to stand out on the solid hills of success to his claim.

Jesus understood this great practical principle. He would erase the systems of the earth with their high and low, pain and pleasure effects. Understanding that in a world where there is the cry of starvation there must also be the laugh of the banquet, he undertook to erase both. With his right hand he parted the curtain of human mind to right and stopped pleasure. With his left hand he parted the curtain of human mind to left and stopped pain. He certainly did this for himself. But his claim is that he has done it for the world. His claim is that he has exposed, not only for his own use, but for the use of us all, a city where they hunger no more, they have no sun nor darkness, they have the uncomparisoned, undescribed, substance.

Whether we know anything about this earthly world, or its inhabitants, or not, need not matter. A knowing can come streaming through us, from us, radiating to limitless areas. This is forgiveness for the unknown. Whether we can do anything by any system of doing now practiced on earth, or not, need not matter. A doing power can work through us, and for us, and by us, transforming every point of the earth. This is forgiveness for the undone.

"He will overturn, overturn, overturn."
"Behold, I make all things new."

Jesus of Nazareth endeavored to surrender himself utterly to the undescribed knower and doer, not only to satisfy himself, but to introduce a new order on earth for all the inhabitants thereof.

He found out that no man, by searching, could ever know anything. He found that no man by working could ever accomplish anything. All wisdom and all works were of the Divine One. So he let the Divine One be his wisdom and do his works, not only to satisfy himself, but to forgive mankind for working and never accomplishing anything, and for studying without ever knowing anything.

Knowledge Shall Be Their Portion

It has been hinted in some quarters that it was the scheme of an ignoramus. It has been boldly stated that he never accomplished the undertaking. This lesson finds men at this point, and declares that their hints and statements shall have no weight. They shall have forgiveness with the rest of the world. For these statements they shall have in their places understanding, and plain handling both with eyesight and fingers, of the undescribed temples and palaces of the city wherein Jesus walks. He got there by claims of knowing nothing and doing nothing, that is, he had absolute forgiveness. And he claims that by his sight and touch of heavenly things all the people of the world are actually seeing and touching heavenly objects every instant.

If they claim that they cannot see heaven around them, under their feet, over their heads, they shall be forgiven for their blindness. They shall be forgiven for their soundless words. They shall suddenly see that they are not on earth but already in heaven. They shall see that the former heaven and earth are passed away. They shall utterly forget them both, and be satisfied with what has dawned upon them.

One does not have to believe that Jesus saw once and forever, and by his sight draws all men's sight. The mission of Jesus was more majestic than that. The instant opens when people see whether they believe or not. It is more comfortable to accept the offer of that one who offered himself for such a purpose, but does not alter the free, universal entrance of all mankind into sight of the great city that now lieth four square here on this earth.

The crucifixion took place on Friday, the day of forgiveness for foolishness, ignorance, incompetency. The trials took place between 1 o'clock a.m. and 8 o clock a.m. April 7. The crucifixion began at 9 a.m., and ended 3 p.m. The Sanhedrin sat in a semicircle, and judged everything in a half light. They always took testimony half way around. There were seventy of them. The evidence against the success of Jesus is always about seventy to one.

He was before Pilate from half-past five to 8 o'clock Friday morning. Pilate tried every way except by direct proclamation of his innocence to liberate Jesus. But he represented the wriggling systems of all time which never permit men to go straight to the divine source for anything; therefore he must carry out his part of the illustration and do nothing. This was promptly forgiven. Jesus told him that he himself gave himself into his hands, and all the condemnation was on himself. Note how he said that he had power to keep himself from imprisonment; that he freely gave himself as a malefactor: that he took all the condemnations of all the world. Nobody should be blamed for what they did not know or had not done. He himself would take the blame.

127

Paul says this is certainly sound scriptural teaching. The golden text of this lesson reads: "Christ died for our sins, according to the scriptures." (I Cor.15:3) If anybody undertakes to make anything else out of the claim and plan of Jesus of Nazareth he finds himself wriggling like Pilate till his head shakes or his heart quakes. He had better read scripture exactly as it says.

The word "Calvary" stands for intellect at its top notch. It is the place of the skull. It is high intellect, capable brain that objects to the Jesus Christ quality. Good reasoning says that each man shall work out his own errors and cram his own brain. Good reasoning says that as there are somber hues in high art to produce fine effects, so there must be sadness on the earth to balance the joy. But Jesus Christ touched a realm where none of such symbology would apply. It was a realm without opposite states. Therefore, reasoning is all useless as related to it.

Reasoning is the crucifixion of Jesus Christ, Crucifixion means hiding. All reasoning, argument, defense of a position, is treason against inspiration. It hides inspiration the instant we begin it.

While one is on the skull plane, sorting out good from evil, and proclaiming the power of good over evil, he can reason. But when he touches the Jesus Christ name he touches the unreasonable and unaccountable.

Deductions to be Drawn

On the cross Jesus Christ was called King of the Jews; that is, the supreme over religious reasonings. On the cross he was accompanied by two thieves, one of whom caught his vision from the light in the eyes of Jesus, and the other of whom took hearsay evidence with the splitting soldiers.

He who caught his vision from the light in the eyes of Jesus began to teach the other one at once. He was so successful that the other did not retort. This is abundant evidence that he was converted instantly.

Confucius went home and kept silent three days when Lao-tse gave him his first information about Tao, the silent, but all accomplishing God. He who keeps his brain from talking with his tongue in the presence of divine information is converted.

The sun hid his face at high noon that the face of Jesus might shine through the ages to come because of his offer to man. The veil of the temple parted to right and left to show the ghost fabric of the skull how to let go. The man Jesus cried with a loud voice that he had found his God-self for the world's sake.

It was like the captivity of Job which we read was turned away when he prayed for his friends who had been making themselves enemies. When our enemies are all forgiven we are at rest. There is harmony everywhere. But though we should sandpaper ourselves with penance for a century

129

and plead with the Almighty like beggars as long as we could gasp, there is no forgiveness in us for them. This lesson proclaims that it was the special offer of Jesus to forgive our enemies for us. Let him handle them. It is the divine self that has something to give to those who knows us not and do not bless us.

Inter-Ocean Newspaper, June 14, 1896

LESSON XII

The Risen Lord

Luke 24:36-53

It makes a great difference to one's religious views to make an honest investigation of the Christian Bible. One gets to really seeing how the writers of it were filled with inspirations from the winds of some realm quite different from the ozones of the atmosphere air enveloping this earth.

They used the tongue and pens of the physical world to tell what they felt metaphysically, and thus they are not to be sympathized with except by such as have felt the same metaphysical influxes.

Last Sunday's lesson gave the most searching power of vision to its readers of any that has ever been written. Like every one of them, of course, it had its plain statement of what constituted the actual doctrine of the man Jesus and like every one of them, of course, it held a secret dart to pierce the inward parts that every reader's mind and life and destiny might quickly "leave their outgrown shells by time's unresting sea."

But in its own unerring light last Sunday's lesson showed up three points of living science and set the Jesus Christ teaching as far away from all that has before been given, even when it has had bodily cure on its wings, as sky whose un-scanned stars meander on trackless plains from earth. A new efficiency stole on its penetrating beams into the heart that read its printed interpretations. Today's lesson is its natural sequence. There could never be any risen Lord in life until last Sunday's chapter had been finished in life. Did it not explain that forgiveness is better than righteousness? Then did it not show that no man or woman ever yet did or could forgive, actually, one who had not understood them and had not done the right thing by them?

Did it not show the difference between being a character who always falls in with the present currents of thought and one who persists in seeing from his own native judgments? Did it not show up the present Christianity of man as a simple sorting-out-of-good-from-evil process not at all like the actual teaching of Jesus Christ?

It has been said that these lessons are slyly leading the mind away from confidence in the Christian Science that has been blooming as the flower of time's efforts at religion. It is to be hoped that they will. It is their openly avowed expectation. For there has as yet been no religion given to man which has not dealt with the power of life over death and given a good reasoning for such a good fight. These lessons do not deal with the battle-ground, where health destroys sickness, pleasure destroys pain, love destroys hate. Once in a while they play with the swords of right and left contests, and show up how the right wing, called good, infuses a lot of ministers to recruit its ranks when it droops, then how the left wing, called evil, scrambles to haul back some of our people to its side when it gets weak.

But their main purpose is to show how to set the eyes of man on a kingdom not identified with life and death. They stand for such a kingdom. They call for the eyes to see, the ears to hear, and the hands to touch the un- describable things of that diviner realm where God, the Almighty, in changeless splendor stayeth. These lessons show the Jesus Chris position. They transcend the first round of the healing religion that has been flourishing now for many years as far as the majesty of fightless victory can transcend the gladness of Napoleon when D'Enghien fell dead, or David when Goliath was beheaded, or you when your seeming rival's voice was hushed.

These lessons touch with their untaught pinions the heights unscaled, but long ago attempted by the prophets and the bards. They wing their unassisted flights to where the searchers after motives and intentions are baffled.

Center on the Atonement

They fly on with un-companioned gaze to rest on the bosom of a motive called atonement. With nothing behind them to prove themselves with, nothing to right or left that confirms them, nothing ahead of them but a promise, they lay hold of nothing, they contend for nothing, and yet know that they are exposure of heaven to the eyesight of man as nothing else has ever been or ever can be. Read them over. They do not ask belief in them. They do not preach faith. They deal with a diviner kindness than a being who asks faith in himself before he can accomplish anything. They do not teach principles. They look upon one who was before the law of thought, before the starting place of truth, antedating eternity and the ways of cause. "A thousand years in thy sight, O Mighty One, are but as yesterday when it is passed, and as a watch in the night."

The golden text of today's topic is, "The Lord is Risen indeed." The topic is "The Risen Lord," or the blessing that now is falling on our heads through the cleft made by one man's touch, and sight and taste of undescribed kingdom. He fulfilled to the letter all the conditions prescribed by inspiration as to how a man might represent all men. He snapped the bands of nature and showed his heavenly face. He cracked the gates of mind and showed his un- teachable glory. He undid the bars of necessity and showed the smiling countenance of everlasting provisions, for which the sons of men need not plead. He stood as a living representative of what the soul of man knows itself to be. No man was ever so sweeping in his purposes. No man was ever so stupendous in his plan. He stood on the untouchable line that spins between man and God, and handed man over into God, dissolving time and human nature in the God substance as a chemist hands over ether into air or air into ether.

That is what he said he did. That is what the scriptures are based on. That is what has not till now been taught, although at the first reading it sounds exactly like the atonement preached by the church of civilization. But the church of civilization is as red in tooth and maw as nature with her carnivora while not the sound of a groan or the sight of a tear marks the atonement set forth by these lessons. No little child ever runs to and fro in a Christian man's employ, no rag picker begs at a church deacon's gates, no tired father is beaten while trying to hold his own.

Something happens that takes away the opportunity for one man to crush another. Something arises that lifts the bruised heart out of the reach of the bruisers. This should never be plainly seen till it was plainly preached. It is plainly preached now. Therefore the Lord is risen. Not the Lord of Life over death, but the Jesus Christ presence in this universe, who in the character of Jesus of Nazareth handed death into life, and life as it is reckoned into something unmatched. There is a life that is not matched up with death. This man touched that life spot, and neither life nor death are counted any more at all by him. Countless eons would not avail to erase the errors of a man on the plane of fighting evil with good or misery with peace. He could not erase evil with right-eousness. Note the doctrine of the Brahmins concerning repeated reincarnations, ages on ages. Sadness increases with them, as ages roll on, and they honestly admit it. But the erasure of errors with their miseries, may be made. The Christian Bible tells of a man's coming who shall do this, and then tells of his having done it. Plato said: "We look for one." Jesus said: "I that speak unto thee am he."

This lesson with its transcendent influences may be found in Luke 24:36-53. The disciples, who had believed that Jesus was God, and then were deeply disappointed that he did not accomplish more, were gathered together after his burial, and suddenly he stood in their midst as alive as ever. They were terrified but he said, "Peace." Then he said: "Why do thoughts arise in your hearts?"

Whoever lets thoughts arise within his heart is certainly subject to misery, because a thought is an ugly taskmaster.

The healing science that is now flourishing takes a handful of thoughts to punish and destroy other thoughts. But such a style of healing never can do anything more than temporarily heal a few bodies. It never changes dispositions. The same

ugly traits that stood up in the first thought train-
ers are still standing up in them. If they
determined to call names and make faces then,
they are still at it.

The Science of Jesus Christ

The Jesus Christ science stops the thoughts
which constitute the disposition. The Jesus Christ
science unrolls first one vision on the eyes and
then another, each vision striking rapidly nearer
the actual. Those scared disciples first detected a
familiar face, then a familiar form, then a new
character entirely. This new man had the power to
open the door of understanding. The other man
had not done this. They had had to train themselves before this in order that they might
understand something. But now all they did was
to stop thinking and watch with their eyes and
listen with their ears to what was happening that
the rest of the world could not detect.

Repentance, remission, forgiveness are again
in his themes, but his name was the name of the
Father into whom they should turn mankind.
They were to keep their minds still, their tongues
still, their legs and feet still till the powerful authoritative "I Am" on the central poise of their own
being had risen up in them, with radiating, ex-
tending efficiency. (Verse 49)

After having it plainly stated that Jesus of
Nazareth worked out the problems of human existence once for all mankind, the only thing to do is
to keep still; keep out of sight; wait.

All the flourishing speakers, teachers, writers, healers of Christianity are evidences of not having had any opening of the understanding concerning scripture, nor concerning the risen Lord. They have not heard the mighty query: "Why do thoughts arise in your heart." (Verse 38)

This new character which Jesus now exposed, had a new disposition. First, in himself, he seemed plainly now to the disciples to be a new power, able to ascend into the heavens, able to bless them with strength, able to change them from carping, gloomy minds into joyous up-borne authorities. (Verses 50, 51, 52, 53)

Then in themselves, later on, they discovered that they were new men; not a trait left like their former incompetent, easily brow-beaten, whining selves. Ability, fiery eloquence, vitality enough to raise the dead, wealth enough to run nations, wisdom enough to silence Kings, strength enough to defeat armies, came suddenly springing up from the secret hot springs where the God spark fired their hearts.

This lesson details the correct directions for those to follow who have read the last year's lessons faithfully. There is no telling how long is the silence between the close of the old dispensation and the opening of the new, but to stop short of both, with thought and speech, that is certainly the way.

"He led them out as far as Bethany, and he lifted up his hands and blessed them." "Bethany" means house of dates. We are stopped in the right place to listen and see. The right place for new blessing. Wherever we find ourselves, there let us quietly remain till a certain harvest is in. Then with gaze still on the point taught by all these last lessons, we find ourselves going back to some city or spot that is in verse 52, Jerusalem. It will be the outward spot representing the return of our life to something like the glory that we had with the Father before the world was, the nearer the return, the more wonderful our imbuement of new inspiration.

Never forget that each of these lessons touches the heart life of every reader in more or less startling measure every week. They set currents going that so many millions are agreeing with, that singly and collectively, that whole world gets their substance. So this week we have no business to be thinking. Above all things, do not think. (Verse 38) We are at the gateway of some change full of blessings. We shall return full of joy to some former abode, both as a state of mind, and as a city, and there, after some days, the new authority will rise within us, enabling us to fulfill the destiny for which we were foreordained, and full of forgiveness for our having tried to do good and great and generous deeds for the world before we had had our eyes opened.

There is no joy so unspeakable and full of conquering radiance as the joy of being forgiven for having worked for the world.

Inter-Ocean Newspaper, June 21, 1896

LESSON XIII

Review

The Bible lessons have been teaching for the last two years that repentance is turning away from existence to face being. It was about the first movement that Moses spoke of when describing the creative power. "It repented the Lord that he had made man on the earth, and it grieved him at his heart." (Genesis 6:6)

This was an excellent symptom on the part of the Lord, or law creating mind. Every one of us has this law-creating mind, so every one of us is a Lord. We can imagine anything and run our mind with that imagination till our bodies are sick. We can imagine a law and feel the effects of it till we get ready to stop. An aphorism is something imagined. Stick to it and it will operate like a machine.

Take this axiom: "Man is born to trouble." Pretty much the whole world believes that axiom. So, pretty much everybody has trouble. But the Bible teaches that man is born to trouble or not to trouble according to his own Lord, or his own way of insisting. "Thou shalt decree a thing, and it shall be established unto thee." "A man's word is his only burden." Moses might have understood what he was talking about and he might not. It is very likely true that he knew about the authority vested in every man, woman, child, for he practiced authorizing and arranging till he could compel metals to change into live things and even ashes to work miracles.

He made up a history of the operations of a man all goodness. He made up a history of a man all badness. He made up a history of a man partly good and partly bad. He made a note of one who would not deal with either good or bad. His histories are perfectly accurate.

Moses knew about how our axioms cover with veils the wonderful kingdom in which we are walking. "What makes a man look like a beggar in rags with no legs and half blind? Why, an axiom. We keep one in the mind and heart which is certain to cover some son of God with the beggar mask. Here is one that will fix up a set of beggars on a great avenue close to some syndicate building: "Self preservation is the first law of life." This axiom gets to rioting around in the subconsciousness of man's mind and finally moves his feet and hands so that he is instinctively protecting himself from something all the time.

He has a family of children to whom he bequeaths that axiom audibly or implied. They flinch and squirm to protect themselves also. Then they breed some young ones who catch the same idea and also flinch and squirm to protect themselves. After a few generations they are begging at somebody's gates as sure as they keep on producing offspring. The descendants of Pharaoh and the descendants of other great kings of the past are examples. Queen Victoria's future descendants and those of our owners of princely fortunes are all hurrying on toward standing armless and legless at some future man's marble fence posts.

All Have Companion Sayings

These axioms all have their companion axioms. This miserable one about self-preservation has a good one which reads this way: "The thing I feared is come upon me." First, beggars come flocking around. They come upon us unaware, they annoy us when we are feeling pompous and rich. Then they descend from our loins. "The Philistines be upon thee, Samson."

But beggary is not the only mask made by axioms. We make Czars and Presidents by them. How Moses declared that the first time any man discovered how he was fixing up the world with conditions and making men in a disagreeable fashion he repented that he had made such a state of affairs on the earth.

Repentance is turning around. Facing the other way. Stopping. To stop with the feet and hands is not the only stopping. The mind must stop too. In the Dhammapada we read that the mind is very unmanageable at first, but after a while can be reined in like a horse. Instead of looking ahead, we then look backward both with mind and eyes. This cuts off our sight of men as beggars and Presidents. Then we are repenting that we have made man. We cut him off. The world cannot exist as a world if we do not attend to it, or to the axioms that have fixed it up. To exist is to stand out. How can a beggar stand out covering up the wonderful soul, if nobody believes he has to protect himself from anything or preserve himself in any fashion?

"For the world grows polar to us, slowly taught,
  Then crystals out a new world,
    like our thought."

This point reviews the first of the last twelve points taken up by an international committee of men, who held good and bad axioms, and have always done all they could to whip the bad with the good. They took for their first point, on April 5, the story of how much wailing and gnashing of teeth there shall be when one man gets the lesson of repentance and stops creating such a whirlpool of creatures as now perambulate this globe. (Luke 13)

The man who has stopped creating with his axioms says: "I never knew you; depart." It seems, by this story, told as an illustrative one by Jesus of Nazareth, that there shall soon be a great deal of scrambling and howling on the part of these fantastic masks we call men when we stop thinking the axioms which made them. But all their howling will do nothing. We have repented, or turned around to see the divine one on his throne at our own head center. We have new business on hand. Finally the masks of all dissolved. The former earth shall pass away, and man shall forget misery has a story of romantic shadows.

Lesson Has Another Title

The committee entitled that Lesson "Warnings." Its actual title was: "It repented the Lord that he had made man."

April 12 they took the story of the great supper and made a picture of a table with people eating bread and calves to show by illustration how much there is to eat if we could only get at it, both of spiritual food and grain stored in western elevators. The story as told by Jesus declared that miracles always happen to every one who stops making masks to hide the mighty kingdom that stretches its beautiful lengths through our airs.

The beggars in the highways throw off their masks. The cripples on the street corners throw down theirs. They rush to the supper. They hunger no more, neither thirst any more. They were formulated by an axiom which being stopped, their rags and hunger must stop. That lesson told how hardly those will take the change who fear there will be no joy left if we cannot have oxen to whip and thrash, land to buy and sell, marrying to scramble after, etc. For the kingdom that lies here at hand has a finished supper which does not represent any money or labor or shrieks. Jesus taught of this kingdom. He did not finish his instructions.

"I will see you again," he said. That was Luke, fourteenth chapter. Its interpretation was April 12.

April 19 told of the two systems of trying to find the throne place, the authoritative center of ourselves. First, the Brahmin dumpiness; second, the Christian activity. Neither has ever been successful, and never can be. It was illustrated by two sons of one man. One stayed at home and kept up a system of good aphorisms. The other ran to and fro, and whirred a set of bad aphorisms. They both had to stop and turn for home. The home in their Father's bosom where they first hailed from. Then they radiated joy like sunshine.

Represents the Third Potentiality

This represents the third potentiality of repentance. First, independence; second, miracles; third, joyousness. All these are radiated from the companionship of one who is repenting.

April 26 told of the different ways of diverting man's self. It was printed in the Inter-Ocean of Monday morning, instead of Sunday morning. It showed that what we have called death does not alter our own dispositions; for the rich man began ordering Lazarus around the instant he caught sight of him. He spoke quite peremptorily to father Abraham, also. But the kind of idea the rich man had fed himself upon while on this earth dining and dancing had brought its fruitage to him in a very hot and disagreeable climate as well as great bodily disorder, while the kind of idea Lazarus had

146

fed himself with had fruited in a most pleasing environment.

The countries in which they found themselves were opposite in nature. It was a season which showed that some ideas don't come into demonstration till after what is called death. One kind is the abstract fear of hell and the other is the abstract hope of happiness.

Tiberius was in mental fear so great that he wrote to his servile senate: "All the gods and goddesses are daily destroying me." He tried pampering his bodily senses to divert his mind. Lazarus had to revel in imaginary blessings to divert his mind from the hardships on this earth. Solomon groaned so loudly sometimes that he frightened his retainers. Lazarus, who represents one who feels hope and sticks to hope, smiled in his sleep sometimes when he had had no supper and Solomon's, or Tiberius', or Rothchild's, or some of those people's servants had kicked him.

Comes Only After Death

These two states of abstract feeling do not have a great rousing environment till after what is called death. It is the law of diversion. Neither is the state preached by Jesus as heaven. The two environments wrapped around Dives and Lazarus after death had to be repented from exactly as the environments of this earth were repented of by the Lord man Moses admired so much.

May 3 showed that faith is an excellent power of mind to make the will topple things over or build them up, but it is not what does the exposure of the God kingdom. It simply enables a man to fight a state of affairs with his mind or will, and overturn it. Jesus did not fight. Jesus did not quarrel. Jesus did not have faith. Jesus had no will. Jesus did nothing. This made him so naked that he finally could not be seen at all but only known as a name.

It illustrated how one set of men cannot accomplish anything unless they have people hanging around who have faith in them. It showed how even God is published not to do anything unless prodded up by somebody's ego. It declared that stones also are in the same condition, but may work like charms if believed in.

Jesus refused to be believed in till he had done his works. This showed that he had an altogether different God from what our pulpits have been declaring. "If I do not the works of the Father believe me not." I do nothing. The Father does everything. I do not urge or coax or threaten or praise him.

It showed up the first Christian science as preached by Adams forty years ago to be a hard pill. It showed up the second Christian science as preached by the healing transcendentalists of this generation to be a hard pill also, for its workers are so overworked by its axioms and formulas and aphorisms that it was only a change from bodily to mental exercising that they had made in their wish to accomplish something to change this world.

It showed how sly it is to tell about loving or serving or adoring God for his own sake. This puts a motive on some high gymnastics of mind. It was primarily an imagination that sounded so fine that some people ran after it, and said it was an acrobatic leap of mind that beat the motive of trying to heal and feed the world.

Paul told the Corinthians to cast down even their highest imaginations.

Forgiveness is Giving

May 10 showed that there has to be forgiveness for doing good to our fellow men. It is an insult to the kingdom of heaven to cover its finished glories over with masks and then declare that the divine original instituted such caricatures and we must fix them over.

Forgiveness is giving for. If we repent, we get a new state. It takes the place of the old. It is not working over masks that is meant by the Jesus Christ life, but repenting and being given sight of the Actual.

May 17 praised the man who never thought of what he could do for God, but only watched God the all-doing one. He seemed to be good for nothing. He seemed to be condemned by the very Almighty he was losing himself in.

But he was the glory of the divine one, for he was nothing — nothing on purpose — and so his divine throne was visible. He disappeared, but the throne one whom he had praised and waited for was left shining in majesty.

It was according to the highest instruction of Moses and Jesus, to let ourselves be swallowed up of our own divinity, letting it do all and be all.

That lesson gave the plain information that it is those who are being condemned and who have no running and preaching and trading to do who are doing all the slitting of the veil that hides the kingdom that now circles around us and the great throne where our Father stays.

Nobody can do so much to dissolve a mask as he who does not look at it, does not think of it, never agrees with the making of it, and has a quality that burns and melts everything he ignores, leaving exposed whatever he notices. This is profoundly metaphysical. It is, however, the simplest of facts, for we always expose whatever we are giving our attention to. We make it more visible than our own personality unless our own personality is the subject we are most interested in. The man who gave up his one talent was attending strictly to the soul of the spheres and spaces. Therefore all the eyes of all men were directed toward that soul.

May 24 showed up the three messages of philosophy already given to the world, but rejected though perfectly true. It showed up the last scheme of the universe to call man's attention to his own soul. This also is always rejected. Yet the soul, which is the great able one, the only able one, shall be visible.

All men shall see it at the same instant. We scold if people do not swallow our enthusiasms about God, or be enamored of our ardor for God, but the least morsel of the actual God they would swallow with gladness. Some clap their hands to catch the God power, some think thoughts to catch the God power, but the centuries skip away and nobody has eaten a morsel of Him. This makes the teaching of Jesus so supernal. He did not clap his hands or his thoughts. He did no maneuvering. He let go of all these. Thus he was the stone of original splendor, without scums of axioms, or masks of belief. That lesson showed how shining is the immovable rock, the soul at its unclothed headquarters.

Like Fleeing to a Mountain

May 31 explained that it is like fleeing to a mountain top of safety to repent. The weighted mind is the mother mind, eating all the aphorisms, axioms, religious teachings, philosophizings, that arise. This mind swallows everything the Orientals tell it and everything the Occidentals tell it. Men often have this mother mind. They cannot think or breathe independently. They have to have guides and leaders. They cannot tell what lightness and freedom comes to those who stop believing the axioms, aphorisms, Bible texts, etc., given them by their neighbors.

They shall rise as on pinions of unburdened light.

It is as enchanting to stop believing anything as to stop carrying a peddler's pack. It lifts up the head of a man to find that in himself he is enough of life, substance, and intelligence to live and breathe. He need not mix with the world in order to handle the world. He has the privilege of repenting from ever having been either a scholar or a philanthropist, both of whom are artificial masks, blurring the unteachable, unapproachable soul. No man can face his soul and keep his scholarship. No man can face his soul and keep his love of doing good. He flees from these weights.

June 7 taught that no man can face his soul and hold a Governor's or President's or Captain's position. He that is greatest must be too near nothing to be trying to govern his fellow men. Then, again, no man can be governed who faces his own soul. If he were in prison the doors would open. If he were commanded to sit on a jury he would not obey. Poverty could not shackle him. Ignorance could not hamper him.

It taught to beware of benefactors. To look far out and help clear of founders of manual training schools, old women's homes, hospitals, etc. They have governing wills in secret, and hold unseen clutches on your life, mind, and affairs. They are unconscious themselves of their secret throttles. Nothing but facing the soul can get us free from the mystic snatches of what are called benefactors.

(Luke 22:25) This is a. hard piece of information, but it is the truth of things perambulating on the mind plane.

June 14 is the banner story of vicarious atonement. Read it over.

June 21 is the final theme. He who touches it with his eyes begins to feel the pull of that unseen magnet whose place is everywhere, whose rule is the rod of the divine magnetic iron drawing with resistless call the attention of this whole people. Its name is the name unspeakable. Its effects are the joys indescribable. Though the kings and the queens and the princes seem to reign, yet who so feeleth the rising draughts of this magnet is out of their jurisdiction. Though affliction and misfortune shade the life, the magnet melts them down. When thy father and thy mother forsake thee, the bands of this magnet will bear thee up.

'Tis ever the rising, ever risen One, with his influence eternal drawing on the heart strings. What wonder that cherubim and seraphim cast down their golden harps and suns and moons stop shining when the bands that draw earthward are proved powerless in the mastering smile of one man as he throws off earth's captivity? How marvelous it is to be free.

Inter-Ocean Newspaper, June 28, 1896

Notes

Other Books by Emma Curtis Hopkins

- *Class Lessons of 1888 (WiseWoman Press)*
- *Bible Interpretations (WiseWoman Press)*
- *Esoteric Philosophy in Spiritual Science (WiseWoman Press)*
- *Genesis Series 1894 (WiseWoman Press)*
- *High Mysticism (WiseWoman Press)*
- *Self Treatments with Radiant I Am (WiseWoman Press)*
- *Gospel Series (WiseWoman Press)*
- *Judgment Series in Spiritual Science (WiseWoman Press)*
- *Drops of Gold (WiseWoman Press)*
- *Resume (WiseWoman Press)*
- *Scientific Christian Mental Practice (DeVorss)*

Books about Emma Curtis Hopkins and her teachings

- *Emma Curtis Hopkins, Forgotten Founder of New Thought –* Gail Harley
- *Unveiling Your Hidden Power: Emma Curtis Hopkins' Metaphysics for the 21st Century (also as a Workbook and as A Guide for Teachers) – Ruth L. Miller*
- *Power to Heal: Easy reading biography for all ages –Ruth Miller*

To find more of Emma's work, including some previously unpublished material, log on to:

www.highwatch.org

www.emmacurtishopkins.com

WISEWOMAN PRESS

Vancouver, WA 98665
800.603.3005
www.wisewomanpress.com

Books by Emma Curtis Hopkins

- *Resume*
- *The Gospel Series*
- *Class Lessons of 1888*
- *Self Treatments including Radiant I Am*
- *High Mysticism*
- *Genesis Series 1894*
- *Esoteric Philosophy in Spiritual Science*
- *Drops of Gold Journal*
- *Judgment Series*
- *Bible Interpretations: Series I, thru XXII*

Books by Ruth L. Miller

- *Unveiling Your Hidden Power: Emma Curtis Hopkins' Metaphysics for the 21st Century*
- *Coming into Freedom: Emily Cady's Lessons in Truth for the 21st Century*
- *150 Years of Healing: The Founders and Science of New Thought*
- *Power Beyond Magic: Ernest Holmes Biography*
- *Power to Heal: Emma Curtis Hopkins Biography*
- *The Power of Unity: Charles Fillmore Biography*
- *Power of Thought: Phineas P. Quimby Biography*
- *The Power of Insight: Thomas Troward Biography*
- *The Power of the Self: Ralph Waldo Emerson Biography*
- *Uncommon Prayer*
- *Spiritual Success*
- *Finding the Path*

Books by Ute Maria Cedilla

- *The Mysticism of Emma Curtis Hopkins*
- *Volume 1 Finding the Christ*
- *Volume 2 Ministry: Realizing The Christ One in All*

List of
Bible Interpretation Series

with date from 1st to 22nd Series.

This list is for the 1st to the 22nd Series. Emma produced twenty eight Series of Bible Interpretations.

She followed the Bible Passages provided by the International Committee of Clerics who produced the Bible Quotations for each year's use in churches all over the world.

Emma used these for her column of Bible Interpretations in both the Christian Science Magazine, at her Seminary and in the Chicago Inter-Ocean Newspaper.

First Series

July 5 - September 27, 1891

Second Series

Third Series

Fourth Series

Fifth Series

July 3 - September 18, 1892

163

Sixth Series

September 25 - December 18, 1892

Seventh Series

Eighth Series

Ninth Series

167

Tenth Series

October 1 – December 24, 1893

Eleventh Series

Twelfth Series

Thirteenth Series

Fourteenth Series

Fifteenth Series

January 6-March 31, 1895

173

Sixteenth Series

Seventeenth Series

July 7 – September 29, 1895

175

Eighteenth Series

Nineteenth Series

January 5 – March 29, 1896

Lesson 1	Missing	January 5th
Lesson 2	Missing	January 12th
Lesson 3	Lesson on Repentance *Luke 3:15-22*	January 19th
Lesson 4	"The Early Ministry of Jesus" *Luke 4:22*	January 26th
Lesson 5	Missing	February 2nd
Lesson 6	Missing	February 9th
Lesson 7	The Secret Note *Luke 6:41-49*	February 16th
Lesson 8	Answered Prayer *Luke 6:41-49*	February 23rd
Lesson 9	Letting Go The Old Self *Luke 9:18-27*	March 1st
Lesson 10	"Me, Imperturbed" *Luke 10:25-37*	March 8th
Lesson 11	Lord's Prayer *Luke 11:1-13*	March 15th
Lesson 12	Be Not Drunk With Wine *Luke 12:37-46*	March 22nd
Lesson 13	The Winds of Living Light *Luke 12:8*	March 29th

Emma Curtis Hopkins was absent on a voyage to Vera Cruz, Mexico to bring her ill son back to the USA. She left December 28, 1895 and returned February 6, 1896. This would account for missing lessons in this quarter. She may have mailed the two in January or they may have been written previously.

Twentieth Series

April 5 – June 28, 1896

Twenty-First Series

July 5 – September 27, 1896

Lesson 1	The Lord Reigneth	July 5th
	II Samuel 2:1-11	
Lesson 2	Adeptship	July 12th
	II Samuel 5:1-12	
Lesson 3	The Ark	July 19th
	II Samuel 6:1-12	
Lesson 4	Purpose of An Adept	July 26th
	II Samuel 7:4-16	
Lesson 5	Individual Emancipatioin	August 2nd
	II Samuel 9:1-13	
Lesson 6	The Almighty Friend	August 9th
	II Samuel 10:8-19	
Lesson 7	Salvation Is Emancipation(missing)	August 16th
	Psalms 32:1-1	
Lesson 8	Individual Emancipation	August 23rd
	II Samuel 15:1-12	
Lesson 9	Absalom's Defeat And Death	August 30th
	II Samuel 16:9-17	
Lesson 10	The Crown Of Effort	September 6th
	I Chronicles 22:6-16	
Lesson 11	"Thy Gentleness Hath Made Me Great	
	II Samuel 22	September 13th
Lesson 12	A Fool For Christ's Sake	September 20th
	Proverbs 16:7-33	
Lesson 13	The Lord is a Strong Tower	September 27th
	Proverbs 28:10	

September 27 of this quarter is a Review of the International Committee listing, not Emma's usual listing and review of the previous lessons in the quarter.

179

Twenty-Second Series

October 4 – December 27, 1896

74233169R00110

Made in the USA
Middletown, DE
22 May 2018